33 : About

By

Steve Schofield
ponderingthought.com

Copyright

2016 Steve Schofield

All rights reserved. This book may not be reproduced in any form, in whole or in part, without written permission from the author.

Cover art by John Hoke_____

Edited by Tricia L. McDonald at Splattered Ink Press

All Scripture taken from the NEW AMERICAN STANDARD BIBLE®, © Copyright 1960, 1962, 1963, 1968, 1971, 1972, 1973, 1975, 1977, 1995 by The Lockman Foundation.
The "NASB," "NAS," and "New American Standard Bible" are trademarks of The Lockman Foundation.
Used with permission.

Acknowledgements

Many thanks to those who shared their testimony including Tamarah Gonzalez, Marv and Tarry Everingham, Kristeen and Joe Hulliberger, and their son Blake and his battle, Shavonne Smith, Barb Vickery, and my parents for allowing me to write and share their journeys inspired by the Holy Spirit. Thanks to my wife for being supportive during the entire book writing process. She is a true gift from God.

Editor's notes

As a two-time cancer survivor, I am leery of people who have never had cancer writing about it. This author caused me no pause. While he admits he has never had cancer and can't speak from that experience, he does a masterful job of capturing the frustrations, fears, interminable waiting, interminable testing, and the unknowns experienced by patients, loved ones, caregivers, and healthcare providers. I expect he wrote a good portion of his book through tears. The book's gift is unabashed hope.

Contents

Copyright _____ 2
Acknowledgements _____ 3
Theme Verse _____ 6
About the Book _____ 7
Inspiration to Write the Book _____ 8
How the Book Finally Got finished _____ 10
My Parents' Journey _____ 12
SECTION 1 – The Beginning _____ 21
    Poem 1 – Command _____ 28
    Poem 2 – Cold Chill _____ 31
    Poem 3 – Convert _____ 34
    Poem 4 – Cloud _____ 37
    Poem 5 – Charity _____ 39
    Poem 6 – Chair _____ 42
    Poem 7 – Change _____ 45
    Poem 8 – Constipation _____ 48
    Poem 9 – Character _____ 50
    Poem 10 – Courage _____ 52
    Poem 11 – Care _____ 54
    Poem 12 – Condition _____ 56
SECTION 2 – A Brief Conversation _____ 58
    Poem 13 – Chains _____ 67
    Poem 14 – Conflicted _____ 69
    Poem 15 – Culture _____ 73

- Poem 16 – City 76
- Poem 17 – Challenge 78
- Poem 18 – Courageous 82
- Poem 19 – Confused 84
- Poem 20 – Comfort 87
- Poem 21 – Conceal 90
- Poem 22 – Chips 93
- Poem 23 – Chuck 96
- Poem 24 – Curb 99
- Poem 25 – Characterize 101
- Poem 26 – Curse 104
- Poem 27 – Cure 108
- Poem 28 – Connection 112
- Poem 29 – Celebrate 115
- Poem 30 – Compass 118

SECTION 3 – *His Ministry Begins, Changes World Forever* 120
- Poem 31 – Chemo 132
- Poem 32 – Caregiver 136
- Caregiver Prayer 140
- Poem 33 – Christ 141

Appendix 143
- Jennifer Longfellow Family Story 143
- Marv and Tarry Everingham Story 150
- Barb Vickery Story 156

Credits and References 157

List of Original "C" words 158

About the Author 160

Theme Verse

The theme verse of *33: About the Letter C* is Job 1:21 (NASB) "Naked I came from my mother's womb, And naked I shall return there. The Lord gave and the Lord has taken away. Blessed be the name of the Lord."

As you read 33, please pray, and when the Lord tests you, remember there are blessings in all circumstances, everything on Earth is temporary. ALWAYS praise the Lord.

About the Book

It's important to set the stage for why this book is written. *33: About the Letter C* contains testimonies describing how Christ was involved in people's journeys with cancer. When each person found out she or he or a loved one had cancer, the lives of everyone involved were changed forever. Unlike previous books in which I was the main participant: I'm an observer in a journey and battle that involves someone close to me, my father James Schofield.

The book also contains stories other people have graciously shared about themselves or loved ones and how cancer affected them. When I asked for their participation, everyone felt it was important to share their stories and the way Christ impacted them in their individual battles. They hope others come to know Jesus and what a difference He made in their lives.

Even in the hardest circumstances, such as battling cancer, everyone can lean on God's word and Jesus Christ's dying on the cross for comfort and guidance. We can have a certain peace of mind while going through the journey, even in times of great stress, emotional and physical discomfort as a result of treatment side effects. This includes caregivers who also bear an emotional burden while a loved one is battling.
Join me in sharing my father's story along with others' testimonies. We want to encourage others through these stories and the God-inspired poems ultimately to bring people to know Christ and the difference He made in the lives of people who were given the task of a difficult journey.

God Bless,
Steve Schofield

Inspiration to Write the Book

I finished the Greenville Sprint Triathlon in June 2013. After a 17-day trip to Malaysia for work, I took some time off after months of training. God encouraged me to take an extended bike ride that included dropping off paperwork at my church. While on my way to the church, the Lord revealed the phrase "It's about the Letter C". I could not stop thinking about that phrase.

Pastor Chuck Davenport and a few others were standing in the lobby. I challenged them to come up with positive, spiritual "C" words. We went back and forth about 20 minutes; the list of C words is in the back of this book.
My first thought was these were titles for another book; I wasn't sure. I was finishing up One Reason: 21 days to a New Beginning, a book based on my training for the 2013 Greenville Triathlon.

I was humbled to realize the letter C stood for cancer. It was a disease three people in my life: my father James Schofield, our worship pastor David Gonzalez, whose story is told in this book by his wife Tamarah, and the third is a co-workers wife. All three received a cancer diagnosis earlier in 2013.

I wondered why God would choose me to write a book on this topic. I have ever been good at struggles nor have I had cancer. The struggle for life is probably the toughest challenge anyone can face. Every time you see a word that begins with the letter "C" in this book, please remember it's about Christ and not about cancer. Christ is the ultimate word that begins with the letter C and the last poem of the book is titled Christ. By no means can I begin to relate the struggle everyone faced. I'm humbled they shared their thoughts with me in the hope these stories would bring others to know Jesus Christ.

How the Book Finally Got finished

I originally wrote this manuscript in 2013 / 2014. How I funded books was not good enough to fund a book until 2 years later. As with previous experiences, the Holy Spirit made it abundantly clear the time had arrived to publish the book. I like to include all inspired information about the book.

A big thanks goes to Ben Fryc for sharing his testimony. During Ben's testimony I kept looking around stating "God, are you talking to me?" I picked up a side job that provided enough resources to fund the book. God uses all his children in different ways and situations, you never know when talking to someone how God might use your situation.

Ben referred to Psalm 46:10 during his testimony. It was about waiting and waiting some more. I related to Ben's struggles about waiting, mine was frustration I couldn't publish my father's story along with others testimonies.

Psalm 46:10 NASB "Cease striving and know that I am God; I will be exalted among the nations, I will be exalted in the earth"

Here are a list of prompts the Holy Spirt revealed during Ben's testimony:

- His testimony like my first book theme verse : Matthew 10:32-33
- He mentioned not my will but God's. Theme verse of my second book : Luke 22:42
- He mentioned 21 days to start a new habit. My third book title 21 days to a new beginning
- His testimony had all things taken away Job 1:21, theme verse of this book
- I've been waiting years for the go ahead to finish this book, God showed Ben through various mediums telling him to wait, same as Psalm 46:10
- The last image on the screen during Ben's testimony was the cover of the book
- Other prompts I got during the week leading up to Ben's testimony
- Earlier in the week, a high school classmate revealed she had breast cancer
- I was reminded of Job 1:21 through multiple items and I had forgotten the theme verse

As you understand, waiting for over two years and having all these items revealed in a short time displayed God's intention. Time to publish the book!

My Parents' Journey

God inspired me to share my father's journey as a battle. Although the components of this journey are not a traditional battle like being in a war zone or a traditional fight, it is a battle nonetheless.

My father is the first to admit he doesn't know why God allowed his body to get cancer. The best I can describe is that God will use my father's experiences to bring others to know Christ. Even though my parents have strong faith and have given their lives to Christ, that doesn't mean they don't have struggles like anyone else.

My parents have been together 55+ years and been involved in probably every situation known to a married couple, yet this was different. Despite a few surgeries here and there, they've had good health throughout their lives. They started and owned successful businesses and raised five kids (which is still a miracle).

As I get older, I ask, "How did you do it?!" In his retired years, my father has gotten involved in farming. If you want to chat about farming, especially growing hay, grab yourself a beverage because it'll be a while. It's his passion and he enjoys it greatly.

Another way to describe my father he is strongly independent, either fixing cars, building something, or starting a new business. He came from the generation that would try anything at least once and would eventually succeed, given enough attempts.

It was January 2013, my father was having issues with heartburn. He made a doctor's appointment to find out what was wrong, and the doctor ordered an upper GI. The procedure determined my father's bile duct to the pancreas and liver were blocked, which was causing pancreatitis. X-rays during a procedure to place a stent showed a mass below his pancreas. Additionally, blood work indicated my father's enzymes were higher than normal.

After further consultation, the mass was diagnosed as cancer. My father had surgery on March 4, 2014. Surgeons removed a softball-size area that included a small part of his stomach, six cancerous lymph nodes, and about half of his pancreas. After surgery, the doctor told my mother and father, "We'll give you a year." That's not the kind of news a person wants to hear after major surgery. The surgeons told my parents that, other than heart or brain surgery, my father's surgery was as complex as it gets.

My mother and father both said almost immediately and openly discussed that "God has a plan." They had no animosity toward God. They were at peace with whatever happened. It was in His hands. One unsettling thing they remember during discussions with doctors was the statement, "This is not curable." The statement's bluntness made them realize the seriousness of what was happening. My father is the closest person I know to have cancer. In his words, "It was a total shocker."

Doctors told him they found the mass early. Being told you have cancer has been described as a kick in the stomach. You never expect it will happen to you.

When the news was communicated to our family, it affected everyone deeply. Thankfully, my father had access to world-class doctors and facilities.

This was just the beginning of the battle to answer questions like:

- Where do I begin dealing with the doctors?
- Is the information provided accurate?
- Why does one doctor say one thing and another specialist says another?
- What about insurance and how does it work with cancer treatment?
- I hear one thing one time, and when I go back, the story changes.

In any battle, communication and information are keys to winning. Satan uses miscommunication and misinformation to create confusion and frustration and to encourage giving up before the battle begins. As one of five children, I was shocked. I wanted to be supportive, but there is no training for this type of battle.

If you are not in the medical field, trying to understand all the information is confusing. Fortunately, my sister Michelle has been in the medical field for several years and understands processes, terms, and how things are generally done. If she doesn't know, she knows how to find out.

Following the diagnosis and surgery in March, treatment began in June 2013. My father had three chemical chemotherapy treatments (inserted into his blood) and then 29 chemo (pill form)/radiation treatments. While surgery removed most of the cancer, some locations required chemotherapy and radiation. More invasive surgery would have affected another blood supply, according to the surgeon, so they could not go farther.

The treatment lasted until October / November 2014. One positive outcome was that chemo treatment did not cause him to lose his hair. Week after week, treatment after treatment, mundane as it was, there was an unknown element because specialists would say one thing and later deny or change the story. It was frustrating. My father's hope diminished as more and more treatments took place.

One day my father mentioned another patient who had nearly all his pancreas removed. Two surgeries and this person was a bundle of energy, full of life and hope. "I'm not one for misery loves company and each journey is different," My father said, "but this guy has barely any pancreas, two surgeries and look at him. I'm not as bad off as I think I am. This guy's pancreas is the size of an egg!"

After the initial prescribed treatment had been completed, my father had a complete body scan to see how the cancer was doing. Unfortunately, some of the cells had grown in other areas. The cells were too small to biopsy, so we waited. The doctors also told Dad they needed to wait before restarting treatment. One bright spot my father found that helped keep his energy up was protein drinks. When he wasn't receiving chemo treatments, a person would never have known he was battling cancer.

Learning, after all the prescribed treatment, months of waiting, feeling terrible during and a few days after each treatment, that he still had cancer cells and they had spread was depressing news. Throughout all the trial and tribulation, my parents' faith remained strong. My father said people would ask him, "Are you afraid of dying?" He would respond, "No, I'm not. I hope to go quickly and peacefully when God calls me home."

During the couple months we waited to learn about the next steps, my father went to the emergency room (ER) on New Year's Eve (2014) with the "shakes" and a fever. My mother called me, my sister, and my brother to let us know my father was going to the ER.

I recall how I felt watching him shake and knowing there was nothing he could do. My father was uncomfortable. Doctors ran tests before giving him medicine for the discomfort and fever. After waiting for different doctors and learning the results of a variety of tests, my father would either be admitted for observation or sent home.

Unlike past visits to the ER for things like the flu or broken bones, this visit was just one more example of a battle with the disease. It was a side effect from chemo and my father's reduced immune system.

As an observer, you get the sense of the daily frustration when visits to the ER bring temporary relief and you know the issue can return. Problems that result from a compromised immune system can cause issues to flare up at any time.

My parents and family sat in the room for a few hours talking, waiting, and surfing the internet (got to love mobile phones). I remember thinking the waiting is probably one of the things a person never gets used to -- unless you are a patient person.

After the New Year's Eve visit, my father was given some over-the-counter medicines to reduce the fever. When his fever went away, his shakes stopped and he was able to return home. The winter of 2014 was one of the hardest and longest winters on record in Michigan. We received the second most snow since they have been keeping records. Being stuck indoors meant more time for my parents. The doctor told them to stay away from large crowds because of my fathers lowered immune system.

There were weeks when my parents stayed home with only my mother going out for groceries. We would call and check but we couldn't visit. For my fiercely independent father, this was a setback and one more example of the battle of patience and sheer will.

It seemed spring would never arrive, but finally in April the weather got better. My parents were able to go out and start doing activities outside their home. Hans and Krista, a couple living in a Christian commune in New York, had visited my parents in 2012. Hans and Krista were deeply religious, and when they learned about my parents' battle, they invited my parents to visit.

My father had been receiving treatment and didn't feel up to visiting. His white blood cell count was down so he was not able to take treatment that would allow his body to recover and would increase his energy.

One of the things my parents wanted to do was visit Hans and Krista, so they planned a trip in May. My parents and some life-long friends drove to New York and stayed a week. It was good to see Mom and Dad get out, go visit, be away from home.

Hans and Krista took them to several sites and my father enjoyed himself. His energy levels were good enough to participate in all the activities. My parents and their friends stayed about a week and returned home. By then, it was middle of May and spring had FINALLY arrived. After six months of snow, there was none on the ground. It was a welcome sight to be outdoors and enjoy fresh air vs. being inside every day.

There was a setback following the trip to New York. My father received treatment and one of the first days following was particularly bad. In his words, "The grave is looking better all the time." He felt terrible one day, slept through most of it, and awoke the following day full of energy. He never knew how long the side effects after each treatment would last.

As things progressed from spring into summer, my father continued to receive treatment on and off. The routine of cancer was every two weeks. On Monday he had blood work, and if his white blood cells are high enough, he would receive chemotherapy. If not, he would wait a couple weeks and start the process over again. This part of the ongoing battle seemed unending. I give credit to my parents' strong faith and never-ending will to live. It's not something you see them bragging about because the battle with cancer is a long, drawn-out test of patience.

The positive thing about missing a treatment was that it allowed my father's energy to remain high. We even planned a fishing trip to Canada to my brother-in-law's family cabin. It is a 10+ hour drive to a fisherman's paradise. You can sleep in the cabin, have breakfast, and walk out to the boat, which is already in the water, and catch fish all day. In this case, it was walleye. My father liked the break from the cancer routine.

As the battle goes on, I appreciate every time I have a question about how to do something and my father is alive and well enough to answer. As we age and our own children grow, watching our parent's age makes us appreciate the wisdom, knowledge, and humbleness they portray. My parents are humble enough to admit their mistakes and to pass knowledge along to their kids and grandkids.

As of this writing (September 2016), my father is full of energy and "has too many things to do to die." As he said, "The doctor gave me 12 months to live, it's been 42, and I still feel good." Besides the numbness in his feet and hands, which drives him crazy, he feels pretty good most times. I attribute his living past the predication to answered prayer, my parents' humble faith and farming.

May those reading this understand the battle my parents are facing, the mundane routine of never stopping chemo, feeling terrible while taking it, and the side effects. Only God knows how long a person will live before being called home. I pray frequently my father is around many years with good quality of life. In my father's own words about how he works through this, "I try not to dwell on it".

Good advice and easier said than done. May God bless his journey and give my parents peace of mind and physical comfort while they are in this enduring battle. If your loved one is facing something similar, please turn all your concerns over to God and let Him deal with it. Don't harbor anything that can affect your efforts to battle this disease.

SECTION 1 – The Beginning

Jesus was born in humble beginnings as described in Luke 2:1-20. I encourage everyone who celebrates Christmas to read the story to their kids and to appreciate that Jesus' birth is the reason for the season. It's not buying presents or stressing over details of the season.

When life-altering circumstances occur nothing else matters. Jesus is all that matters. Here is a story by Tamarah Gonzalez telling her and her husband David's story.

Cancer, Corruption, and Clouds by Tamarah Gonzalez

THE BIG "C"

When I first heard the phrase, I immediately thought 'Christ' until I learned they were referring to cancer. I thought, 'It's not so big because Christ is definitely bigger.'
We sat across from the doctor as he rather bluntly said, "Cancer, stage 4, palliative" I saw the blood drain from my husband's face as our enemy took on a new form and new name. I'm a left-brained problem-solver, and I immediately formed a plan of attack in my mind as the doctor continued speaking words I did not focus on.

Once the doctor left the room, I turned my heart toward David. He seemed like a soldier without orders as he sat in bewilderment. I held him as we cried. I assured him as my covenant partner that his enemies were my enemies and that I would fight for his life with all my being. Through the tears, we verbally reconfirmed our faith and trust in Adonai of Hosts. No matter the outcome of this battle, He is praiseworthy, He is sovereign, and we will win.

It was Valentine's Day when we left the hospital with a prescription for chemotherapy. The most the doctors offered through chemo was less suffering but no extra time and they made it clear there was no cure. Chemical poisoning certainly didn't sound like less suffering. I realize that many people have survived cancer using conventional medicine, but in this story even the doctors admitted that statistically this stage of lung cancer presented no survivors.

Corruption

This was a devastating blow not only to us but to our church family as well. David's gifts and talents as a worship arts pastor brought an energetic passion to the ministry. His sensitivity and genuine compassion for people cultivated many heartfelt relationships in the three years we had been there.

I served in the prayer ministry and had testified to the numerous and miraculous answers to prayer that God had given our church. It seemed that Mr. Worship and Mrs. Prayer had taken a hit on the front lines. Unexpected? Not really. We were accustomed to the regular artillery attacks of the adversary. We always responded to the fiery darts the same way, with worship and prayer.

This weapon called cancer was different. We had seen its effect on many saints before us. It's a weapon that not only attacks the body of the victim but also the minds of believers rallying around their wounded. It had left a trail of confusion and doubt in the hearts of those who prayed the promises. The question inevitably raised is, "Why?" Why do bad things happen? Why did God allow this? I believe the answer in part is found in Romans 8.

Romans 8:20-21(NASB) "For the creation was subjected to futility, not willingly, but because of Him who subjected it, in hope that the creation itself also will be set free from its slavery to corruption into the freedom of the glory of the children of God."

Since the fall, creation, the Earth, and man have been subject to futility. Futility in Greek means "what is devoid of truth and appropriateness; perverseness, depravity, frailty. In other words, suffering. In increasing measure we are experiencing the effects of sin. Weather phenomena, sickness, disease, crime, broken relationships, and hate are all the futility suffered while on this earth.

These things happen to us because we live in a broken world that is in slavery to corruption. There are many reasons why bad things happen, but it all comes down to the corruption of creation: tornados, hurricanes, floods, droughts, and disease as well as the choices of fallen man: drugs, alcohol, chemicals, driving, airplanes, guns, knives, fire. As long as we live on this earth, which is temporary, we are subject to its corruption. But there is a promise within this Scripture.

Romans 8:18-19 (NASB) "For I consider that the sufferings of this present time are not worthy to be compared with the glory that is to be revealed to us. For the anxious longing of the creation waits eagerly for the revealing of the sons of God."

The apostle Paul in his second letter to the Corinthians writes to the very subject of suffering and seemingly the question of why.

2 Corinthians 4:6-10 (NASB) – "For God, who said, "Light shall shine out of darkness," is the One who has shone in our hearts to give the Light of the knowledge of the glory of God in the face of Christ. But we have this treasure in earthen vessels, so that the surpassing greatness of the power will be of God and not from ourselves; we are afflicted in every way, but not crushed; perplexed, but not despairing; persecuted, but not forsaken; struck down, but not destroyed; always carrying about in the body the dying of Jesus, so that the life of Jesus also may be manifested in our body."

2 Corinthians 4:16-18 (NASB) – "Therefore we do not lose heart, but though our outer man is decaying, yet our inner man is being renewed day by day."

For momentary, light affliction is producing for us an eternal weight of glory far beyond all comparison, while we look not at the things which are seen, but at the things which are not seen; for the things which are seen are temporal, but the things which are not seen are eternal.

We must not set our minds on the things of Earth but rather on the rewards of our future heavenly home. Jesus told us that we would have tribulation, trials, hard times in this world but to take heart because He has overcome this world. Our time on Earth is less about our life here and much more how our life here affects our life Eternal in His Kingdom.

I like to think of our time here in military terms. We are on mission. And there is a war with ongoing battles. The first battle being for our soul: whose side are we on? The enemy does his best to keep us "of the world" so that we don't even put up any fight. The Creator woos us with His love, grace, and mercy to allow Him to be King of our life and be part of His Kingdom. The real battle begins when we surrender our life to Him.

It is then that the enemy employs many tactics to try to discourage us to NOT believe the Truth. The enemy persuades us to believe in what we see. His weapon: lies. The Truth: we walk by faith and not by sight. Our adversary, if he can't convince us to leave our position in the Kingdom, will at least try to rob us of rewards for faithfulness awaiting us in the life to come as well as keep us from being effective for the Kingdom.

The apostle Paul in 2 Corinthians 4:18 (NASB) said "for this momentary, light affliction is preparing for us an eternal weight of glory". In Romans 8 he said "suffering of this present time are not worthy to be compared with the glory that is to be revealed to us"

David's battle with cancer was a painful one. It did drain us emotionally, physically, and mentally. From the moment he was saved, however, he had lived his life for others, and this fatal disease was not going to change that for either of us. It invigorated both of us to continue to minister to others during his last five months.

I don't believe we should set our focus on comfort and pleasure in life. Yes, we can have those things, but if we remember we are soldiers on active duty, our main focus is on our mission, namely, saving the lost, carrying our wounded, and finishing well.

We don't fight against flesh and blood but against powers, principalities, and evil forces of wickedness. The enemy enjoys the distraction of our stopping to question our commander and chief about why He didn't answer our call or respond in the way we wanted.

Clouds

Mark 13:26 (NASB) - "Then they will see THE SON OF MAN COMING IN CLOUDS with great power and glory.

Revelation 22:12 (NASB) - "Behold, I am coming quickly, and My reward is with Me, to render to every man according to what he has done.

Although a wounded soldier, David continued with his mission and mine. We prayed, worshipped, and encouraged others. We never wanted it to be about us but about Him and His glory. Having our minds set on things above sure beat dwelling on the temporary affliction. Suffering does not have to be a waste or for nothing. Neither does death win when it comes to the disciple's door.

For the child of God, we simply move to a new "house" and receive our rewards. "...for this momentary, light affliction is preparing for us an eternal weight of glory." Cancer or any tragedy does not seem to be a "light affliction," but compared with the glory to come it will prove to be a vapor.

In His kindness and wisdom, He orchestrates a scheme for every trial or affliction to work together for our good. In other words, it's an opportunity to respond as a faithful soldier and trusting child and gain spiritual growth and eternal rewards.

When Paul says "our good," that means our affliction does not only work for our personal good but also for the good of others. In fact, the spiritual implications can be limitless. The Lord says that His ways are above our ways. In church we frequently recite, "God is good all the time, all the time God is good."

We must steadfastly believe that, especially in painful afflictions. Faith is the substance of things hoped for and the evidence of things unseen. In the end we did win. We stood steadfast, honoring our King who will reward us in His Kingdom to come.

Let the afflictions of this world and the Devil fuel your fire for the King. Let the suffering spur you on to make the enemy's wiles counterproductive through worship and prayer. Praise Him when your heart is heavy, praise Him when you are in pain. Respond to trials with wrestling prayer for the lost. Keep your eyes fixed on Jesus and imitate Him. Even in the darkest, weakest moments of our souls, our hearts can quietly embrace Him because His love never fails.

Poem 1 – Command

Scripture : John 8

Poem

It is all in how you say it
If you use a stern voice
The command will sound harsh
If you use a timid voice
The command will sound weak
If you laugh while you say it
People might not take you seriously
If you smile while you say it
People will be put at ease
How you talk, the tone you use
The way you give and receive commands is a gift
For some, receiving a command is easy
For some it is not
I tend to take a command personally
Then ponder for a while until I worry
I did this more when I was younger
Not so much these days, there are times though
I have to remember the commands God gives in the Bible
These are the commands I should focus on
Do not worry, Do not doubt
The enemy can't read minds, but can read body language
Once the enemy detects you are unsure or stressed
They think you are trapped and continue to whisper doubts
Be humble, be forgiving when stating a command
Remember Jesus used grace and truth when stating a command

He used this over and over in the Bible
He would state a command, fair and firm
When people were stating a command to him
He would be humble yet truthful
Remember, Jesus was in control of all things
If He gave the command, Heavens armies would have come to his rescue
As I ponder, the next time I state a command
Remember Jesus and how he would state a command
It was not how the culture did it
Sharp, unforgiving, uncompassionate, and hateful
It was loving, humble, patient, and kind
We all need a reminder now and then
How to give and receive a command
Just remember how our Savior did it
This will make you smile
And patiently wait for the next command

Amen!

Story Behind the Poem

I was tired from working on several difficult things. A statement came across as sharp, without compassion during one of the difficult situations. The situation had already been forgotten by others involved, and yet when I pondered more, I was giving the enemy power over me.

The story in the Bible about 'casting the first stone' (John 8:7) is Jesus' example of stating plain truth. In this Scripture, His words are clear. This situation inspires another emotion and brought out a fear of "not being accepted". The way people interact with each other is critical to feeling wanted. If we perceive a command incorrectly, it can make us feel threatened.

I regained perspective after a few hours. I was reminded how I reacted when I was younger. My hope is one day God uses my gift of writing to be more compassionate, not to speak commands so sharply.

Non-believers have a different view of the world. Their motives and how they express a statement or phrase can be different. As Christians, we are commanded by Jesus to love our neighbor as ourselves. When someone says something harsh, our first response should not be defensive. That is not showing love if we respond negatively. When we are instructed to do something, be slow to anger, be humble, patient and kind as our Heavenly father talks about in James 1:19.

Poem 2 – Cold Chill

Scripture : John 18:28-38

Poem

Ever had a cold chill go up your neck?
It happens all of sudden
One moment things are fine
The next you feel a cold breeze
You feel a cool sensation come over you
It makes your body shiver
At first, you retract
That is our natural reaction
I'm not sure if it's for our protection or not
It takes a moment to recover
You sit and reflect a bit
Do I enjoy the cold?
Sometimes people can project a cold chill
Their attitudes are subtle
The feeling of a cold shoulder from someone is the same
You sit and ponder, what did I do?
We are not quite sure how to react
Should I worry over nothing
The other person is probably not worrying about it
Only you sit and wonder why
We are told not to worry
When we do, we give power to the enemy
Although the enemies' home is hot beyond description
Their intentions are to foster a cold chill towards others
It creates doubt and fear, this emotion is unique
We want to feel accepted by others

We don't want to be something we are not
Maybe, it is a phase and it'll pass
I'm not sure how to proceed next
Maybe I'll consult with another person
It is biblical to not harbor feelings towards your neighbor
In times where you feel a cold shoulder
It is time to hand these thoughts over to the Lord
Ask for guidance in helping not to obsess over the situation
If there is something wrong
It will soon pass
Warm your heart, place your fears in the Lords hands
He'll soon help you realize your fear is unfounded
I've been on the walk with the Lord for a while
These old feelings crop up from time to time
It's amazing things from our youth resurface
We sit in doubt, feeling left out
We are never too old to feel this way
The one difference we realize is the Lord is there to help
Thank you, Lord, for your warm comforting examples
How to bring us in from the cold

Amen!

Story Behind the Poem

I was involved in a situation I wasn't sure about how to handle. It bothered me that I might have offended someone and caused me to worry. When I was younger, I had a desire to try to fit in with whatever group I was associated with. This caused me to sacrifice my morals to try to receive someone's acceptance.

When we worry, we are opening ourselves up to attack from the enemy and creating an idol. The Ten Commandments tell us we should not have ANY idols before God.

When you feel a cold shoulder, stop and think it's probably not you or something you did. Don't let something linger in the mind's eye. The other person has probably forgotten about the situation.

Poem 3 – Convert

Scripture : Acts 2:38, Matthew 3:1-11, Acts 9

Poem

We live one way because that is what we know
Day after day, year after year
We go about our business
Doing what we think is best
One opportunity leads to another
We grow in our field of choice
Our goal is to make a name for ourselves
Make a difference within our sphere of influence
This can take us on travels near and far
We go about our merry way
One day, a person crosses our paths
We notice something different about them
They intrigue us and we don't know why
When this person is around
We take time out of our busy lives
To get to know this person
The more we know, the more we are interested
Life continues on and we don't think twice
Time passes by and this person becomes important
We care for this individual
Although our primary interests are still around
They have expanded to include this person
Then...one day a simple question is asked
They ask something that goes against what we believe
Or thought to believe, in the everyday hustle
This type of question never came up

Do you believe Jesus is your Savior?
It's a straight forward question
You either do or you don't
For a person who has been living her or his life without Him
It makes them feel uncomfortable
They first deny it, thinking this person asking the question is crazy
One question and your attitude toward this person changes
You wonder if they are crazy, lost their senses
In your resistance to convert
You leave room to explore their point of view
Your heart likes this person and gives them a chance
You travel half way around the world
You can't escape the feeling of the question
You get back and explore the opportunity
The Holy Spirit won't let up
In your words, the "Hound from Heaven" is after you
You attend a few church services
Skeptical at first
Back to that question, it was the turning point
The Holy Spirit came around, there is a plan for you
At the time, you don't know what's in store
All you know the feelings are different
The adventure begins, what you started out believing
Is vastly different, you are not sure the outcome
You have converted from the inside out
When you accept Jesus as your savior
He'll convert your feelings, no matter if you resist
We all start and end the same
In the middle of the race, those who accept Jesus' gift
Will make a difference His Kingdom!

Amen!

Story Behind the Poem

I read a story about a news anchor who, by her own words, never included Christian activity in her life. For details of the story, here is the link.

http://www.christianitytoday.com/ct/2013/november/fox-news-highly-reluctant-jesus-follower-kirsten-powers.html
What interested me in the story was her honesty and realism. She said. "But you don't know what you don't know." Then she added, "How could I have missed something I didn't think existed?"

For my walk in Christ, it's been one thing after another, and I can relate a little to the "Hound from Heaven" statement mentioned in the article. My second and third Christian devotional books are specifically about being focused on tasks God gave me.

This story reminded me it's not our job to do God's job. Leave the changing of someone's heart to Him and the Holy Spirit. Don't get caught up in God-less chatter or distraction the enemy promotes. American culture is caught up in what's trending and willing to give an opinion on any topic, especially on social media or news sites.

I believe the person God chose in this article is similar to Saul (who eventually became Paul) and his conversion on the way to Damascus. When the good Lord has a plan for you, it's almost impossible to resist. In the end, you'll realize His way IS the better way, even though you lived thinking differently.

Poem 4 – Cloud

Scripture : Matthew 24:30, Mark 13:26-27, Mark 14:61-62, Luke 21:25-28

Poem

Ever seen clouds on the horizon
Before a storm or where a Low and High pressure meet?
They mirror what mountains look like
The shapes are breathtaking
Clouds are represented in various forms
Sometimes they are soft and fluffy
Sometimes they are dark and intimidating
Regardless of the description
They can be used in different ways
Cloud can be used in descriptions too
A cloud of doubt
I'm not sure of the outcome
I have a shade of doubt
What causes shade, clouds can
I once was on a plane flying home
It was a partly cloudy day
When the plane was above the clouds
It was amazing the shade they created on the ground
Clouds can appear to make sounds
Ever been to an airport on a cloudy day
Before you ever see the airplane
You hear the rumble coming from the clouds
God's word mentions Jesus will descend on a cloud
I wonder if it's going to be something like that
The Bible states he'll ride on a cloud with power
There is no doubt it'll be something to witness

The enemy will no longer be able to cloud an issue
Create distraction, doubt and fear
John describes in the book of Revelation
A new Heaven and new Earth will come
There won't be darkness nor anything else bad
Eden will be restored, makes me wonder though
Were there clouds in Eden?
I don't know, one thing I do know
God the Father, Jesus, and Holy Spirit will be there
Only clear blue skies for eternity

Amen!

Story Behind the Poem

I was driving to work one day and drove by the high school my kids attended. I had this feeling about a huge cloud of fear, doubt, uncertainty and something rather unsettling happening. Although the institution of learning is full of well-meaning Christian people, the nature of public education prevents them from fully teaching the Bible as an option.

This opens the opportunity for the enemy to move in and provide options that can eventually create an attitude not favorable towards Jesus. I felt the need to pray and ask for protection. I'm not sure if this made a difference. Only God knows.

Secondly, I learned about a job opportunity that provides "cloud" services. The more I learned about the position, the more I was interested and pursued it. I won't know for a while whether or not I got the position. All I know is when I prayed if I was supposed to interview for this position, the word cloud came to mind. God uses totally different examples in my everyday walk to inspire poems.

Poem 5 – Charity

Scripture : Matthew 10:42, 1 Corinthians 13

Poem

Servicing needs, helping others
Giving of time, selflessness
Donating items or talents for a worthy cause
Helping those less fortunate
Does it mean the less fortunate are unable?
Have you asked the question?
Do you inquire before serving?
Do you already assume to understand?
Have you ever had surgery?
If not, do you know of someone close to you who has?
Were they able-bodied before the procedure?
Did they have a hard time accepting charity?
Good intentions are one thing
Making real change or impact is another
When it comes to solving problems larger than life
Only God is capable
He calls us to be willing
He calls us to be ready
When that time comes, do you think of the other person?
Do you stop and empathize or sympathize?
Jesus talks we'll always have the poor among us
In our world today, that statement is very true
There are needs all over the place
Next door, a town a few miles away, and around the world
How we serve the needs are different
Some are immediate and fulfilling
Others are longer term

No matter the task, we need to listen to God
Many get lost thinking we know best
We do the thinking for God
Instead of letting Him lead us
Remember dignity, integrity and respect
Love thy neighbor, helping them shows love
Sometimes, it's a cup of cold water
We don't know the true outcome of our efforts I believe
God talks about treasures in heaven
Better to invest in something that doesn't disappear
Eternal investments reap the best rewards
Better to come along side someone
Than think you know best
Having God lead the charge
Will definitely cause change, no matter the circumstance
Let God define how He'll use you in charity
You might not know the cause
He wants the willing and able
To do His work
Leave your pride at home
In the end, you'll be surprised the outcome

Amen!

Story Behind the Poem

This story is based on a couple different items. The first one comes from the book called *Toxic Charity: How the Church Hurts Those They Help and How to Reverse It by Robert Lupton*. It was a thought-provoking book that tries to make people involved in charity think differently when "performing charity." I had mixed emotions about reading it because one of the examples mentioned was "events that pick up trash."

I coordinate an annual project to pick up garbage before my towns annual festival. My second devotional book (*Remember the Nails : 40 Days Doing Something Uncomfortable on Purpose*) was inspired by picking up trash.

The intention was for people to get out in their neighborhoods, pray for people who live there. Pickup up garbage was the vehicle God used to get people involved. Anyone involved in compassion or community-based ministries or projects should read *Toxic Charity*, it'll sharpen your perspective. I don't feel it's my call "yet" to perform the ministries Robert talks about although I like his direct, as-a-matter-of-fact approach. When doing charity, make sure to think of the other person.

Secondly, a good friend offered to drive me to the doctor for my checkup after a double hernia surgery. It was an opportunity to be the recipient of assistance (you could call it charity), it was humbling, and it provided perspective between being the person performing charity and being a recipient.

Accepting charity and assistance from others can be hard. Regardless whether you are the person doing the charity or the recipient, ask yourself if it's done in God's name and love is shown, does it matter? I'm glad God showed me this lesson and book because they helped provide some perspective from both sides.

Poem 6 – Chair

Scripture : Proverbs 3:5-6

Poem

Chairs are objects we use to sit in
This is a pretty common fact, they have been around forever
Many items can be used to make chairs
A log, a piece of steel or leftover parts
A chair can take many shapes, sizes and forms
Some are larger, some are smaller
Some are more comfortable than others
All have the same intention
To provide a place to rest for a while
It can be eating, watching television, or sleeping
Have you ever been trapped in a chair?
Did you ever need help getting out of a chair?
What did people think when you asked for help?
Was it humbling to ask for assistance?
You have been getting out of chairs your whole life
It's something you take for granted
You don't give a second thought until you can't do it
Ever had something you always did taken away?
What were your thoughts?
Did you realize "What did I get myself into?"
Until we can't perform them anymore
A chair is one example God uses to help us realize
It can be used for comfort or be trapped in
Either way, it's a simple reminder
Don't depend on your own understanding,
it is best stated in Proverbs 3:5-6 (NASB)
"5 Trust in the Lord with all your heart

And do not lean on your own understanding.
"6 In all your ways acknowledge Him,
And He will make your paths straight"
The next time you take something for granted
Remember, God is involved in all things
The big, the small, and in between
That is God reminding you gently to rely on Him
Thank you God for using such a simple object as a chair
To help remind us
Don't take simple things for granted
And lean on you for all things

Amen!

Story Behind the Poem

I had double-hernia surgery and for the first few days, I slept in a recliner. I was unable to get out of the chair without assistance. On the fourth day after surgery, I woke up at 5:20AM, no one was awake besides me. My son had just left for work. When I tried to sit up, I felt a sharp pain like needles poking me in the stomach. I realized I was helpless, I started to have racing thoughts and had a panic attack. The medicine contributed to the panic attack and things did not get any better.

One of the things I thought about over and over, "I cannot undo this surgery and what did I get myself into?" Could I be permanently disabled? I couldn't even get out of the chair. Many negative thoughts went through my head. It was not a pleasant day.

I had taken Xanax to reverse effects of the anxiety, I felt like a walking zombie. I took several naps and when we had some friends visit, I was not a very good host, to say the least. The Lord gave me this example and Scripture to write about. I had been praying about how God was going to use the surgery to give me more stories to write about. And on top of it all, it started with the letter C.

Poem 7 – Change

Scripture : Job 28:12-28

Poem

Some can be positive
Some can be negative
Change can just be something different
Whatever level it is
Something will be altered
It could be a haircut
It could be a new job
Requiring you to move
Not all is bad
Not all is good
Change in itself is just change
Nothing fancy, just something adjusted
There is one entity that doesn't change
God, He is constant
Past, present, future
He has always been, outside the boundaries of time
Time always changes
Time is man's invention to measure
In a human's lifetime
Change happens constantly
People resist it, we can't get away from it
During the process, people are uneasy
One way to ease our worry
Is to turn over our change to Him
God cannot be measured
He is eternal past, eternal present, and eternal future
Eternal is forever

It has no beginning and no ending
No change, nothing altered
God's wisdom is holy, unchangeable
Through His son Jesus Christ
We can change for the better
We can change our course to become eternal
It's such a simple thing, accept His free gift
Make Him Lord of your life
Change will be for the better, forever

Amen!

Story Behind the Poem

There are a few things that cause us to get uneasy. Change, for example. At the time God laid this word on my heart, my church got a new pastor who had been under constant change for three years. He is married with four small children and making a career change. We were at a party and his fortune cookie included the word change in it. It was a bit ironic.

Secondly, I had a few things changing in my life at the time of this poem. I had recently undergone surgery to fix two hernias, it was the first official surgery I experienced, and it was definitely a change to be restricted for several weeks. Having constant discomfort was a change in my life because I couldn't just do what I wanted.

Next, I accepted a new position at work that was quite a change in position and responsibility. It was still working in information technology, but in a new area. When I got back from medical leave, the change surprised many people. Unlike job changes in the past, the change for me wasn't as drastic as what others thought.

Lastly, while reading the Book of Job, I was reminded how his life went through many changes allowed by God. In Job 28:12-28, a question about wisdom is asked. As our lives change and we get older, wisdom becomes more and more something you cherish. I recalled, "I seek wisdom from the one who created wisdom."

For a layperson, this means, "I seek God's wisdom over my own." Amazing how God used different examples to help inspire this poem. If you have a change going on and you read this, I hope you hand it over to God. He'll help you through it regardless of whether it's simple or not.

Poem 8 – Constipation

Scripture : Genesis 32:22-32, 2 Corinthians 12, John 16:21, Romans 8:22, Isaiah 13:8

Poem

Life has a way of backing up
We get so busy, we forget to do the basics
Then one day, your routine is interrupted
This uncomfortable situation not allowing you to sit, stand, or sleep
When you are in the middle of something
This is when the unexpected happens
Before this, you would never have guessed
Consistency on a daily basis keeps things moving
Good habits such as diet, exercise
It's so simple, yet many overlook the obvious
This can potentially impact every person
At some point in his or her life
Good habits help prevent this dreadful situation
During rough times, we tend to pray more
God asks us to bring our worries, fears to Him
Most people forget in a relationship simple things matter
Giving thanks, showing appreciation, doing stuff for others
God made us to have a relationship with Him
His word says so, don't let your life get so busy
It interferes with spending time with your father.
Jesus died on the cross and was uncomfortable
A lot more so than any temporary pain we might feel
God, thank you for helping me realize
My temporary discomfort is yet another reminder of the simple things

Praying often is like eating every day
It can help keep things consistent in your physical as well as spiritual lives

Amen!

Story Behind the Poem

I had double-hernia surgery, and a few weeks later, when my weekend started I felt terrible cramping and couldn't sit, stand, or sleep for 36 hours. I thought it was food poisoning because the symptoms were the same. I went to the hospital for treatment. Hernia surgery prevented me from pushing while "doing the business." Of all the topics I've written about, this is probably one of the most "uncomfortable" (pardon the pun) I've shared. God helped me realize my discomfort was temporary.

If you've had surgery and taken pain meds, you might have experienced constipation. When I talked to people about this topic and had surgery, they stated "Yeah. I have constipation. It's not fun." The poem shows, in a funny example that it wasn't fun at the time. We need to be consistent in praying and giving thanks in all situations. God does have a sense of humor.

Poem 9 – Character

Scripture : Psalm 12:7-8, John 16:33

Poem

Something goes wrong
You desire to walk away
In your heart, you know leaving is wrong
You just want the pain to go away
Moment after moment, you seek relief
Anything to help with the ache inside
This ache is not physical, but mental
The positive feelings you once had are gone
Our culture says you don't have to work through issues
There is a pill for that, an alternative or so they say
A quick fix to your problem is what we are promised
There is nothing too hard that can't be fixed
If it's too hard
Just quit and start over, regardless of the consequences
There is one thing that you can't quit in God's eyes, Marriage
It's a bond between a man and a woman
They become one when they say I do
One flesh doing life together
There are times of adversity that can test one's character
Left to ourselves, we'll fail miserably without God's help
"Lord, I pray for today's youth starting out
They have grown up in a media-rich culture
They are told you can have it your way
They can quit if they don't like it, no matter the consequences
Working through adversity creates positive character
The challenge helps a person mature
May you lay your hand on those who need a lift

May they be humble enough to listen, learn from your word
As they work through the issue
The hope is they learn and grow stronger
We know the outcome if they don't stay
There will be heartache and pain
It doesn't have to be this way
Your word is clear, lean on you
Through your son Jesus
There is no challenge too big
If they just lay their problems at your feet
Father, thank you for challenges that build character"

Amen!

Story Behind the Poem

I was reading about a young mother and wife. She mentioned to her husband about not being happy and wanted to leave. Divorce was the easy way out. Today's culture promotes the idea we don't have to work through issues. When I typed a response to this individual, I included a prayer and also mentioned adversity creates character.

Life is not easy, marriage is not easy. There is more pressure than ever, especially on middle- and lower-income people. This can create the desire to quit and walk away; it's someone else's problem. No matter your age or experience, there will be challenges. No one is immune. Jesus said you'll have trouble in this life but "fear not because I have overcome the world." John 16:33 : NASB The story was a good reminder to leverage God in any and all things we struggle with. His Word says so.

Poem 10 – Courage

Scripture : Joshua 1:9

Poem

Uncertainty arises in many forms
From a health issue to a new job or learning something new
Each situation provides an opportunity to grow
For some, the first instinct is retreat
While going through the challenge
Most people don't have any hope of success
They are JUST trying to avoid failure
Some cringe at the thought of something different
As they gain experience
Some gain confidence, some continue to fail
It takes courage to continue
Regardless of immediate success or continued failure
When walking through a tough situation
Humans have two choices: continue or quit
Most will try many times before giving up
Until someone succeeds at the challenge
Most people observing an individual today
Will discourage rather than encourage
To help with failure
We put up barriers trying to protect ourselves
Some can be physical
Some can be with a negative attitude
Until a trustworthy person comes alongside you
Trying to do something alone takes courage
Take time to reflect on a situation
Do not measure your progress as success or failure
Look at the situation as an opportunity

God gives us many of those in our lifetimes
We have free will to accept the challenge
Courage is God's gift to help overcome fear
With God alongside you, nothing is too big
God will patiently wait for us to take the first step
We gain strength and knowledge through failure
With God's help through prayer, we gain courage through the unknown
Regardless of the size of the challenge
Life will have many hills and valleys, each step takes courage
Don't go at it alone
God is there every step of the way.

Amen!

Story Behind the Poem

My father was fighting cancer and we didn't know whether the treatment would help. He completed one round of treatment, which seemed to help, but in the final evaluation, more cancer was found. He had two choices: refuse treatment and likely have a short time to live or try more treatment. Another friend from high school also had cancer. Her final diagnosis was a clean bill of health. Another lifelong friend had a stroke and was recovering. Each individual's attitude was courageous.

Secondly, today's culture tells us to be politically correct. This can cause people to be cautious and not courageous because there could be backlash. Both situations require courage although they are completely different. The one common bond is Jesus and seeking His wisdom, guidance, and assurance based on scriptural examples. Knowing God's word can help in times that require courage.

Poem 11 – Care

Scripture : John 2:13-22, Luke 15:1-7

Poem

People can have passion for ideas
Passion brings out honesty
Honesty is truth in a passionate person's eyes
They want to pursue their dreams
When you feel strongly about something
You promote it, you let us others know how you feel
When you interact with people who feel differently
Your passion can collide with their ideals
When two parties disagree
This is an interesting paradox
One party feels strongly about their position
The other party has an opposing opinion
Differences are okay as long as they are done respectfully
Today's culture teaches everything is okay
Everything is subjective
Everything is right, nothing is wrong
This creates ambiguity
People are not sure what is right and wrong
One day, one thing is right because the culture says so
The next day, this idea is wrong and people make fun of it
The minority making the most noise gets the most attention
They have passion and care for their ideas
Is it right? Depends on how right and wrong is measured
For centuries, people have used God's Word
Mankind tends to be selfish
We want our ideas, thoughts, and actions to be right
This can change, God's word does not

God's word has passion, it's very deep
The more you study, the more truth is revealed
Sharing God's Word is a passion for some
When this goes against the culture
It creates a difference of opinion
Jesus stated one day you would be persecuted
For those who claim He is their Lord and Savior
We are on this Earth for a short time
We have a choice to make, choose the culture or choose Jesus
My passion is for Jesus, I've experienced His grace
He died on the Cross for me
I can't imagine how much Jesus cared for His flock
His passion to do the right thing is unmatched
Jesus, thank you for showing you care about your people
You showed us how to care and have passion!

Amen!

Story Behind the Poem

I've read articles over the years that have promoted different ideas, thoughts, and positions on a variety of topics. Things have taken a shift so minority groups get the majority of the attention. This leads to advances for some agendas that impact the majority of people even though the group is a small minority of the population.

This has impacted basic society rules and behaviors. Regardless of the topic, neither side of the debate can agree on common ground. This happens in our federal government with the division from our leaders who can't seem to do their jobs. There is passion on both sides, some preach tolerance yet do not live it out. Do as I say, not as I do is the example. Regardless of the position, you can express love and show you care even though there are differences.

Poem 12 – Condition

Scripture : John 16:33, Philippians 4:12, Luke 2

Poem

The Holy Bible states to be content in all things
That is easier said than done
There are occasions where unknown things occur
Uneasiness creates anxiety, we wonder about the future
For those who have accepted Christ
We know our future
We know what our condition will be
Although the uncertainty is not easy right now
Finding peace in unsettled times brings perspective
Whether the day is cold, cloudy, and terrible
Or is bright, sunny, and peaceful
Seek the Lord and all His good no matter the situation
If you are experiencing something unknown
Take time to lay it at God's feet
Jesus mentioned we will have troubles while on Earth
He mentioned "Fear not, for I overcame the world" John 16:33
The unexpected can become expected
The result can remain unknown
Our faith in one name, one Lord is certain
We know our condition when we accept Him
Lord, I pray for everyone no matter their circumstances
Some have health issues, mental challenges, and other things
By saying a few words, I accept your free gift
You came to Earth, the Word became flesh
You accepted the conditions although you are holy
You took on our sin for all time, for all people
For those who don't recognize that

Please have them realize it
Whatever they think of Christians
Please have them love Christ
Accepting Christ will change your condition and position
Lord, I thank you for all conditions, all challenges
In an eternal view, our condition is set
We don't have to be concerned
While on this side of Heaven, when things get tough
Help us through our condition to be more like Christ

Amen!

Story Behind the Poem

We experienced an especially cold winter (2013/2014), lots of snow, no brief thaws. This made people tired of winter and ready for a change. I'm not sure what the weather is like where you live, but in Michigan, the winter of 2014 was especially tough. The day I wrote this story, instead of doing my normal devotionals on my way to work, I let the Christian station play and I sang. I wanted to follow the Spirit. If you are experiencing something while reading this but you don't know your condition, please review John 16:33, Philippians 4:12, Luke 2. I hope it helps you find peace and comfort in the Lord.

The Condition poem does a good job of describing Jesus's situation when he came to Earth. He was in Heaven, Holy and Perfect. He accepted other conditions to take on man's sin and correct things by showing His love.

SECTION 2 – A Brief Conversation

Jesus' early years were not documented except for one instance when he was 12 years old. (Luke 2:41-52). Cancer can impact everyone young, old, and in between. Kristeen Hulliberger was gracious to document her son Blake's journey. Here is their story told in their own words with answers to starter questions I asked everyone who shared their story.

What kind of cancer did you have?

Pre B All (acute lymphoblastic leukemia) Cancer of the blood unlike adult cancers, it is not known why kids get cancer. While most adult cancers come from lifestyle choices such as smoking, childhood cancers are different from adult cancer even though some are named the same. For example, leukemia is very different from and treated differently for kids than adults.

What kind of treatment did you or your loved one have?

Blake underwent many different treatments from chemo IV to chemo pills to chemo shots to radiation All the chemotherapies affected him differently, and most of the time we would skip to the worst-case side effects with him. He did not take the chemo well. The Vincristine gave him seizures, the PEG shot gave him a stroke, and the spinal taps with Methotrexate gave him swelling on the brain.

It was not always the cancer we were fighting. Often we fought the side effects of the treatment. Because Blake's immune system was low, he would often get sick. Meningitis put him in the hospital for two weeks fighting for his life with massive headaches and neck pain.

He also got Parvovirus, which made it look as though the cancer was back and his body was not building red blood cells. As a result, he underwent a year of treatment fighting this virus with a blood plasma product and IVIG meds as well as high doses of steroids for two weeks to offset the side effects of IVIG.

Can you describe your feelings and emotions when the doctor confirmed you had cancer?

A peace above all understanding!!!!

What kinds of things are you doing to help yourself to relax or find support?

Our wonderful pastor's wife would come to the hospital and we would run the track outside the hospital. Her talks, wisdom, and hugs helped me. Many tears were shed during our time together, but the time with her always helped refresh my soul to keep moving forward.

Members of our church made dinners for our family. This was such a help when we would come home from the hospital. It helped in so many ways because it was a burden lifted and we could enjoy more time together.

My family helped with the other two kids, Paigelyn and Dylan, who stayed with Grandma or bounded between their aunts' houses. It was so hard on them, but having family there to help was a godsend.

During the journey, do you recall times when you questioned God and His plan?

It's funny, but it was not until later on in the journey that I did! After Blake relapsed I felt more angry and helpless. I knew then what we were in for and that the journey would be much harder with more intense chemo. I remember Pastor Joel telling me It was okay to ask God why. For some reason, before that time, I felt it was not. I just had it in my head that God had this and I never felt as though God gave this to Blake, but that He was trying to heal him.

Were there any Scripture, songs, or music that you leaned on for comfort and strength?

This is a funny answer and the truth is the song that got me through is the country song "If You're Going Through Hell." I remember singing it a lot.

How did your relationship with Christ change?

In the beginning, the change was very close to God. I felt drawn closer and closer and then somewhere along the line I felt my heart had hardened. Not that I had any anger but a sense of knowing this world is full of horrible things.

Children are dying every day, and I have been surrounded by the horror of watching children throwing up, crying, and screaming from getting poked. I have been to too many children's funerals of friends we met at the hospital. I feel overwhelmed sometimes when I am around people who complain about their day. I want to scream and say, "You have no Idea what a bad day is!"

One day that sticks in my mind is one spent at the clinic (the outpatient cancer center at the hospital) and it was a rough day for Blake. When I got home I needed to run to the store to pick up more meds for him, and I remember two ladies going at it in the aisle about how horrible their day had been and their jobs. I found myself staring at them with tears in my eyes thinking, 'Do you have any idea where I spent my day? Watching small children fighting for their lives hooked to a pole to get meds or blood or chemo to hopefully save their lives.'

I wanted to just scream at them, but God reminded me EVERYONE is fighting a battle. Just because theirs are different from mine does not make their battles any less than mine. WOW! That hit the heart and I have tried very hard to remember that.

Anything else you would like people to know?

It always amazed me that when a tragedy hits, some people thrive, others pray, and others run. New friends replace the old scared ones. I don't think it's because they want to but because some people are stronger than others.

One thing for sure as a result of this is that when you know someone hurting or sick you don't call and ask if they need something! They don't know what they need most of the time but they need you. Just show up, make a dinner, send a card, and be a true friend through it.

I had no idea that Blake's treatment would put us on a constant journey for five years and for the rest of his teen years! He will need assistance the rest of his life, but I know God has an amazing plan for this tough guy.

Blake's Story by Kristeen Hulliberger

It was July 2008 and everything was wonderful. My husband and I were celebrating our 10th anniversary and our son Dylan was celebrating his seventh birthday. We had our own cleaning business that was growing fast and doing well.

We had a new home, Joe's work was going great, Paigelyn was about to start middle school, and Blake was more than ready to begin kindergarten in September. Blake and Paigelyn were playing around. Paigelyn was trying to take Blake's ice cream from him when Blake fell on the corner of the table and hit his ribs.

Later that night, we took him to the hospital in Greenville to have his ribs checked. Blake's ribs were fine but he had an ear infection, and the noted that Blake looked very pale. They put Blake on an antibiotic and sent us home. During this time, Blake was playing T-ball and getting very tired out. We thought he must be fighting off the ear infection.

As the week went on, we had Dylan's birthday party and then Joe and I left for a night in Traverse City to celebrate our anniversary. When we got home things were about the same. We had planned a camping trip with our kids so we left for Pentwater. It was a hot day on the beach but Blake was very cold. We wrapped him in a blanket to keep warm.

When we got home, Blake went right to bed. When he woke in the morning, the lymph nodes in his neck were swollen. We called the doctor's office right away and headed for Grand Rapids. We told the doctors what had been going on and the doctor ordered blood work to see if Blake might have mono. After the blood work we took him home. About 10:30 p.m.

Our doctor called Joe and told him Blake was a very sick boy and that he had leukemia, Blake's white blood cells were higher than they have ever seen. The doctor told us we needed to get him to Helen DeVos Children's Hospital right away and that they were waiting for us.

When we got to the hospital, it was so scary. There were tests and they kept trying unsuccessfully to put an IV into Blake. We were taken to the seventh floor where we would talk to Blake's oncologist and hopefully get the answers we longed for. Blake had Pre B ALL., He was diagnosed at high risk because his white blood counts were so high, and, he had less than a quarter of his red blood cells left. They were going to give him a blood transfusion.

The doctor explained that the first two weeks were critical and that Blake's bone marrow was full of cancer. We started chemotherapy right away and learned Blake's type of cancer has an 85 percent cure rate. As cancer goes, it is the best one for kids to have. Within two weeks he was doing a little better.

They gave Blake a PEG shot the night before we were to go home. Immediately, Blake had massive headache and his legs hurt so badly from the chemo attacking his bone marrow. The doctor ordered a CAT scan that showed nothing to worry about. We took him home the next day and he just laid around all day. Something was wrong!

We took him back, and as we sat in clinic, he had a stroke. He went in for an MRI, and we spent the next six weeks in the hospital with him. Blake's liver was failing, and he needed platelets, plasma, and red blood over those weeks. His immune system was at zero and we were in a fight for his life.

Somehow through all of this, the peace from God was over us. (God had given us a peace above all understanding.) Blake would go on to have numerous problems with chemo: swelling on the brain and seizures. The Vincristine took some of his motor skills. The stroke affected him more than we ever knew. He lost everything: numbers, colors, and letters. We had to start over with him. His visual memory was weak and he faces a multitude of learning difficulties from now on.

Two years passed and Blake was doing well. He was on a maintenance phase of chemo with mostly home chemo and once-a-month visits to the hospital. He had just started second grade when his cancer relapsed. They did a biopsy and we were right back at the beginning.

This time Blake would have to undergo radiation therapy along with intense chemo. There would be more hospital stays and it would be two more years of treatment. It hit us all like a ton of bricks. We had thought the end was in sight and it was like hitting a brick wall.

Blake has reacted well to treatment and we are currently looking at being finished with chemo in September 2013. After four years of chemo, the effects will last a lifetime, but we are very blessed to have him with us. Through this journey, I could not tell you how much people have opened their hearts to us. Our church stood by us every step of the way.

Our family and friends were there in a heartbeat in the middle of the night when Blake would spike a fever and need to go to the hospital. So many people made dinners for us. When we found out Blake would need special schooling, the outpouring of help blew us all away. To everyone who is taking this journey with us, thank you for being there.

Blake has been out of treatment for a year and a half now although he still gets his blood checked every three months. Life will never be the same for Blake, who will struggle the rest of his life to read and do small motor skills. He has numerous aches and pains from the lasting effects of all the steroids he has taken over the years. Blake will have hormone shots ever day through his teen years. We are so grateful to have him here with us every day.

Childhood cancer is growing fast. Every day 46 kids in the USA are diagnosed and seven will die. Overall, one out of five children who have cancer will die from it. With some cancers, one out of five will live. In a single week, that is almost one of Greenville's elementary schools. Childhood cancer is a huge problem that is overlooked. The national budget for cancer is $4.6 billion but childhood cancer receives less than 3 percent.

Harsh chemo treatments are leaving our kids with lifelong complications. Relay for Life fundraising helps kids like Blake go to Camp Catch a Rainbow. Last summer there were more than 100 kids at the camp. All of you who support Relay of Life are going to be part of this wonderful gift.

There are so many ways you can get involved with childhood cancer. Volunteer your time, be a mentor, be a camp counselor for a week, tell someone about childhood cancer, make dinner for families fighting cancer, do something to make a difference. Give blood regularly.

I did not know the day before Blake was diagnosed that he would need so much blood product, and I am so thankful someone gave blood before we got to the hospital that night. Get on the bone marrow registry. It is so easy. A swab of the cheek and they can start to match you with kids or adults who are fighting cancer and need bone marrow transplants to survive. We all know someone who has had cancer, is fighting cancer, or has died from cancer.

Poem 13 – Chains

Scripture : 2 Timothy 4:1-6, Acts 16:16-40

Poem

Chains of success, chains of failure
Chains of worry, Chains of Anxiety
Chains of lust, Chains of evil
Chains of money, chains of greed
Chains of guilt, shame and sickness when we sin
Another link to our emotional chain is added
Things get heavier, things become harder
We get depressed, we become cold
We forget how to love
We become critical, judgmental towards others
The emotional chains become a burden
They become a debt we can't repay
We carry our chains around every day
For some, the chains become too much
The consequences impact others in many ways
Divorce, more debt, death, murder, many serious things
The enemy can't shake his chains
He tries to trap others
Jesus came from heaven to take on bodily form
He understood the chains mankind has
When he died on the cross
He took on every kind of emotional chain
There isn't a sin, an emotion or situation he didn't know
All sins, for all people, for all time
Do you feel like you are chained up?
Are you stumbling in life from your chains?
Jesus already broke these chains

He is greater than any kind of chain, emotional or physical
Regardless of the situation
He understands and loves us
His sacrifice allows us to break free from our chains
Hand over your chains, give everything to him
It's not easy because there is baggage left behind
Be honest with Him, don't be subtle
Jesus holds the key to eternity
He knows how to unlock or break any chain
He knows how to set us free
No matter the situation, No matter the circumstance

Amen!

Story behind the Poem

There was a testimony by a person who shared about their loved ones who were killed by their spouse and parent. The spouse killed her husband and one child. There were no explanations, no words to describe why it happened. There are many chains today described as discrimination, hatred, bigotry. It's all a distraction, people living in sin masking it in the name of love.

Many people are shackled both physically and spiritually, forgetting how to love and show compassion. They use emotion, they judge others who speak the truth of God's word. My heart goes out to people who are blinded by their sin, hopefully they will accept Jesus' love before it's too late.

Poem 14 – Conflicted

Scripture : 1 Corinthians 8:9-13, John 2:1-11, Ephesians 5:1-21

Poem

There are times in life
When you have a choice between two things
Both choices are right,
Only one is better
Free will is a gift from God
His example of love for His children
Mankind gets to use our brains to make decisions
We can use scripture as a guide
Jesus taught by using parables
They show right and wrong
The view expressed by Jesus is holy
Some of the parables are not quickly understood
It takes time, experience, and patience to follow them
On this side of Heaven, we are ignorant to many facts
Although we seek and learn many things over our lifetime
Nothing can change the fact we are human, sinners at best
We all fall short of the glory of God
Regardless of culture, background, race, or other descriptions
We are given choices, free will to choose
God gives His examples
We should do everything in our power
To learn His holy ways and learn from His examples
God's Word is divinely inspired
Many men have tried to understand the Scriptures
They are called theologians
These are men and women who have an appreciation for God

They were conflicted in their beliefs and expressed their point of view
Entire denominations were created from their writings
Depending on your point of view
Some were conflicted
Regardless of the topic, act with conviction and clear conscience
When a tough choice has to be made
Spend time in prayer, talk with others
The choice is between you and God
The decision will be reviewed on the Day of Judgment
The choice to take the easy way out could be the right way
The harder path could not be realized until reaching Heaven
Our selfish, free will souls tend to select the path seen vs. unseen
Lay your conflicted choices at God's feet, ask for His direction
The answer is never fully realized in our lifetime
Do not let the conflicted choice
Stand in your way

Amen!

Story Behind the Poem

When I became a member at my church, there was only one type of membership. From what I could find, our church started to have two types of members (covenant and community) When our church migrated existing members, each person was selected to be a covenant member instead of community by default.

I learned about the change while serving on the local board of administration (like deacons and elders). Covenant members choose not to drink alcohol. I have a social drink or two every so often. Scripture doesn't prevent drinking, all it says don't be a drunkard or in some cases, don't cause a weaker brother to stumble. If someone has drinking issues, I definitely don't cause temptation. 1 Corinthians 8:9-13

This particular decision has created division within the church because only covenant members can serve on the board, vote for pastors, and so on. I struggled with this for a while, spent time in prayer seeking God's guidance. This was something between God and I.

Depending on your point of view, the right choice is to take the higher road and appreciate what Christ did for us on the cross. There is scripture in which Jesus turned water into wine at a wedding, and Paul talks about having wine to settle your stomach. This leads to the conflicted choice.
I struggle not to become legalistic (aka religion), follow defined set of rules made by man that might not be scripture based.

My hope as you are reading this, if there is a decision that has to be made in your life, you will consult with God and ask for His direction. The choices could both be right, depending on your point of view. Select the one that honors Jesus Christ and helps with a clear conscience on your part.

After much prayer, and time I chose to not feel yoked by the decision that is conflicted with the leaders of the Wesleyan denomination and have adult beverages every so often. Other denominations view alcohol consumption not the right thing to do. Some people might not understand although this caused a conflicted situation. Prayer was a big help in my case.

Poem 15 – Culture

Scripture : Book of Ephesians

Poem

Since sin entered the world
The culture has been changing and evolving
As with anything
If enough people want change
Society changes the laws to fit its fancy
This is regardless of what God's Word says
One day a view can be accepted
As time goes on, this view can change
The culture accepts the change
Even though it could be wrong in God's eyes
Regardless of the topic, the message is the same
Mankind is selfish by nature
When good things are happening
The selfishness doesn't come up
When challenged and backed into a corner
Negative, selfish, and hurtful words are spoken
God preaches love keeps no records
Love does not judge, only lifts up
There are no human words to describe God's love
His Holy Scripture is the best description we have
Many don't understand it, so they don't follow Him
The next time you feel like judging
Remember you are not the Creator
Only that right is His
The culture will change
The Holy, inspired Scriptures will not
Stand firm in your belief

Do with compassion, love, and patience
The culture of the day preaches tolerance
When the culture is challenged, tolerance won't last long
You'll be called names, sued, and even jailed
Jesus died for all mankind
In the culture today, it's more important than ever
To pray for every one
Display truth with love to those who might not believe
Our heavenly Father loves everyone
He wants all His children to spend eternity with Him
Be in continual prayer for your fellow brethren
One day the only culture that'll matter
Will be in Heaven, with Jesus Christ our Lord

Amen!

Story Behind the Poem

I struggle with negativity and judgmental nature of today's online comments and impact on our culture. Christians are called bigots and are hated for expressing the truth of Jesus Christ. I've had my fair share of instances in which I try to express God's point of view and fail. The next time something happens that appears to go against God's word, show love and respect towards others. We are all sinners and fall short of the glory of God.

Here is a prayer I shared on a random post where God's word was challenged.

"To my fellow brethren. Although today's culture preaches independence, Our Lord God through Jesus Christ preaches interdependence on Him, his Father and Holy Spirit. We all love you and want you to enjoy an eternal life with Jesus in one-ness with God, the Father, and providing light forever. Our main concern is not to judge, but to let you know we love you beyond words and want you to share in the good news of Jesus Christ.

"Although human words are expressed and perceived as negative, our hearts yearn to have you know the love, peace, and knowledge our Father God loves you more than you know, expressed by sending His son from the heavenly realm to Earth with humble beginnings. He died on the cross for all men, and although men's hearts can be evil toward one another, the love of Jesus Christ toward his sheep is endless and fulfilling.

"The next time a person feels judged, slighted, or challenged in thoughts, actions, or deeds, please realize the people expressing God's Holy Scripture have a good heart and want you to know the love of Jesus. May God bless your journey, my fellow brethren, and may you realize His love is endless and He wants you to be part of the body of Christ, of which Jesus is the head."

Poem 16 – City

Scripture : John 3:16, Revelation 21:4-8, Revelation 22:3-7, Isaiah 65:17-24

Poem

There is a city not of this world
It is not paved with gold or created with human hands
It's a perfect city where only the holy are invited to live
It's an eternal city created by God, the creator of all
The only thing required to enter the city
Accept Jesus Christ as your Lord and Savior
There are no complete words to describe this city
There are no pictures, only brief descriptions in the Bible
There are also accounts from people who visited
Returned to Earth and tried to describe with human words
Although the accounts are awesome and describe something wonderful
They fall short in describing its true beauty
The Jerusalem on Earth today was home to God's temple
He would dwell with His people until they were distracted and fell away
Jerusalem is the capital of the world
No one has officially claimed that title
Described in the Bible, many things happen and will happen there
I want to be a part of this city for eternity
When you have a moment of peace
Close your eyes, picture this city and you are a part of it
This can help us find comfort on this side of Heaven
Regardless of the challenge you are facing, things are temporary

God, I want to be a citizen of the new Jerusalem
Regardless of the struggle, disease, or challenge
My soul belongs to you, mark me a place
Build me a palace I can stay in forever
It's the only city I want to truly move to
And be a permanent citizen, with all my fellow believers
My prayers go to mankind, my family
My hope they want to go there too and live forever!

Amen!

Story Behind the Poem

I had an opportunity to visit Jerusalem when I was in Israel and it felt like home. My goal was to see the current Jerusalem before the new one comes to Earth as God promises after the return of Jesus. I've read an account in Heaven is for Real and 90 minutes in Heaven that describe parts of Heaven. Our senses are expanded beyond description to enjoy things like heavenly music and worship of our father.

There are struggles in life along with different seasons we go through. Some get married, have kids, have a career, and experience many things. Often there is a struggle and sacrifice to achieve a goal that really isn't all that great once it's achieved.

When we focus on Jesus, there is an actual city we are going to dwell in. Our choices on Earth determine whether we get a chance to live there. I want my choices to reflect my desire to live and dwell in the house of the Lord forever!

Poem 17 – Challenge

Scripture : 1 Timothy 3, Book of Job, Philippians 4:10-23

Poem

When faced with something difficult
The options are few
One can face the difficulty
Or one can run away
For a short time
Ignoring the problem might seem easier
Until the problem catches up with you again
You really have no choice
The decision to face it will bring more challenges
It will test your faith, patience, and will to live
The first questions are obvious
Why me? Why now? Why this? Now what? Really?!
Many of the questions have no immediate answer
Some will never be answered
When facing challenges
You find out who your friends are
Many will be scared; many will abandon you
They don't know how to handle the unknown
They run away from the challenge
Thanking God they aren't facing this themselves
The challenges and daily routine can be tedious
Hurry up, wait, wait, and wait some more
Waiting for this result
Wondering if this treatment is the cure
Sometimes the cure never comes
Sometimes the cure eventually is found
Regardless of the challenge

Having faith and an eternal view can help
Faith, family, and friends are important
They can help through the mundane times
Tragic news is hard to accept
It's the waiting that is almost as challenging
If you know of a person facing a challenge
Don't run away, pray for them, cook for them
Take time to visit, a phone call, or just to chat
Don't JUST ask for an update on the person's condition
Have a conversation
Tell them about your day
Some are stuck in isolation
Some can't venture out too long
Isolation and loneliness can be as bad as treatment
The physical pain from treatment can be unbearable
Combine that with physical and emotional things
This can test a person's faith and resolve
Don't take small things for granted
These will matter more than you realize
When the challenge seems impossible
Involve God, Jesus, and Holy Spirit
When we walk into eternity
The reward is beyond words
Just like the challenge you or a loved was given
May you find peace, comfort, and rest in God
Even though that might seem impossible at times
Reflect, remember, and continue the journey
He might not answer the way you wished
He will answer and be there when needed

Amen!

Story Behind the Poem

Reading *The Books of the Bible* (ISBN : 978-1563206603), my small group read the entire New Testament in 40 days, I learned a good portion of the first half covers Paul's letters. His advice and direction have a godly yet humble perspective. The challenges he faced were described in detail and include the many times he was beaten, stoned, and nearly murdered.

Many people would not continue their faith and preach the word facing these challenges. I find comfort in Paul's instruction, yet there is more to be faced. Some of his instruction challenges me to the core of my being and tests my faith.

Like many of the stories shared in this book, some of the challenges seemed impossible. I once heard big problems need big answers. After getting to know the individuals who shared their stories, I learned big problems need small and simple answers.

Many small, simple answers will help solve big problems. God's Word is filled with many small, simple instructions to help through any situation. When the answer is unknown, we are instructed to lean on Him for all things because sometimes He is the only answer. Although we don't see Him physically in human form, He is present.

I'm humbled God put me on this journey even though I don't know where it'll lead, what it'll impact, or who it'll help or inspire. Even after writing as many stories as I have and revealing my inner thoughts, fears, and ideas, I still long for this 'simple, final' answer. How will these stories help and who will it impact?

I realized while typing this that simple things like everyday conversation and taking time to chat beyond asking for a simple update are valuable even though some people might not see it that way.

Poem 18 – Courageous

Scripture : Joshua 1:9, Psalm 27:1,1 Corinthians 16:13,2 Corinthians 4:7-11,2 Timothy 1:7

Poem

Contemplating the easy way out of a tough situation?
Probably not the best idea
At the time
It makes the most sense
How we handle the change is important
There is an initial fear that can be long-lasting
What if this? What if that?
Thoughts race through your mind
The more you think
The crazier it sounds
The feelings can be overwhelming
What am I doing this for?
You seek advice to reassure yourself
The decision is made to move forward
You can either resist or embrace the opportunity
How you react is important
The decision could have eternal consequences
Some might say it is no big deal
They are humble when acknowledging the feat
Many small decisions help lead to a big result
If you do this with the Lord's help
You are not alone
The enemy reminds you otherwise
It takes being BOLD in your actions to be courageous
After you sit and reflect
Do you realize the courage it took to change

If it was meant to be
There is a sense of peace
If not, you continue to adapt
You do not give up
You continue on the journey
Hope you find comfort in the Lord's example
He descended from Heaven
To be born in a manger, live a humble life
What He did during His three years of ministry
Was the most courageous and humbling thing ever
All He had to do was think
I've had enough, I'm going back to Heaven
Thank you, Jesus for showing the ultimate example of being courageous
We can seek your wisdom and direction
This can help through the scary times
Our faith will one day lead to sight
The first sight in Heaven will be Jesus
The fear of the unknown will be forgotten
We will have joy in the house of the Lord forever
Our faith will have its rewards
We just need to be courageous in the meantime
Seek the Lord in all things!

Amen!

Story Behind the Poem

In our culture, the wave of dissent toward God is obvious. So many Scriptures describe in clear detail the culture is going against God's word. Here is a saying that was laid on my heart. "It was once bold to declare you were AGAINST the good Lord through your word and actions. In today's culture, it's bold to declare you are FOR the good Lord through your words and actions."

Poem 19 – Confused

Scripture : Genesis 5-10, Matthew 13

Poem

There was once a perfect garden
For those to dwell in and rest
All day, every day was paradise
They had enough of everything
They worried for nothing
God's grace abounded in all things
God loved us so much
He granted us free will
We were free to choose
He provided us a choice to stay perfect
Was it temptation or a gift?
The serpent slithered ever so quietly, planted an idea
Did God say not to eat from that tree?
The enemy created doubt, confused the clarity of the garden
Nothing too crazy
Just enough to cause them to wonder
Free will was a gift to mankind
It was God's way of showing love
Mankind chose to tempt fate
They realized what good and evil was
They were cast from the garden
Paradise was lost on Earth
Lost, confused, and 100 percent human
They knew what consequences were
Every day brought doubt, worry, and confusion
Nothing was as before while living in the garden
God set His plan in motion to redeem us

Through his Holy Scriptures it describes how
Though mankind was still confused
The day arrived when His son came to Earth
He was on Earth for 30 years before starting His ministry
For three short years, He traveled and preached
Wherever He went, He preached with clarity
He preached the Kingdom of God was near
His words were as clear as a mountain stream
Pure, simple, and straight as an arrow
There was absolutely NO confusion in His words
Mankind had a choice to follow His son
After all this time, God was still showing His love
No confusion, love my son, and accept His gift of forgiveness
Spend eternity with the Father, His son, and Holy Spirit
No confusion, just a straightforward message
Mankind invented religion which caused confusion
Many are blinded to the true grace of God
The Scriptures state many will call on His name
Not all will enter Heaven
My hope is for all to understand the clarity in Jesus' words
No confusion, no doubt
No matter the challenge or what happens in life
No matter the timing or obstacle
Don't be so confused by mankind and religion
God loves us beyond our comprehension
He doesn't want us confused
One day, we'll return to paradise with Jesus at the helm
It will be clear sailing into eternity
For we will not be confused
We dwell in the house of the Lord forever
No doubt, no confusion, just peace and love!

Amen!

Story Behind the Poem

This story was a mix of things going on in my life at the time. We went to see a movie based on Noah and the Flood. The movie was not accurate from a biblical perspective. It created confusion and doubt, and the media sensationalized the director, a proclaimed atheist.

When the movie ended and we were getting ready to leave, I overheard a couple state this was not accurate and they were going to go home and read the Bible or double-check the Bible. I forget the exact phrase.

This brought clarity about how God was going to use this movie, even though it was inaccurate, to move people to have a conversion about Him. God will use all things for good. Although many will doubt my take, I believe only when we are in Heaven will we know the outcome of some things. I can't wait for the day to walk into paradise, greeting Jesus, and having no more confusion, doubt, and worry.

Poem 20 – Comfort

Scripture : Psalm 27:13-14, John 16:33, 2 Corinthians 1:3-4, Ps 42:11, Psalm 23

Poem

Earthly comfort is different from eternal comfort
God provides comfort to those who seek Him
This might not be what it seems
The expectation is to be comfortable and without struggles
This implies no challenges on Earth
Scripture talks about not loving anything on Earth
Earth is temporary
Heaven will be permanent for those who believe
This will bring permanent comfort
Mankind seeks permanent comfort while on Earth
Although we get temporary relief
We are soon challenged and want more
This brings discomfort to those who seek more comfort
It never ends, we want, we achieve, and we want more
Comfort is an idol without knowing it
We need refuge from our struggles
Just when we think we've achieved victory
Discomfort shows up again
We continue until we give up
The enemy likes when we give up
He first promises comfort
Only to really want your obedience
At first, obedience is comfortable
Until you realize you are uncomfortable
Then you are caught, uncomfortable forever
God's mercy and grace are comfort

Even though it might seem uncomfortable at the time
When we slow down enough to reflect, evaluate our situation
God's comfort is brought into loving Him first
Then loving your neighbor
We should try to spend our lives achieving those first
When we find comfort in the two greatest commandments
We'll find what can be as close to permanent comfort on Earth as possible
Only when we walk into eternity will we find permanent comfort
Everlasting, whole, perfect comfort
That is what I long for and that day will come
When my faith becomes sight
When I see my Savior Jesus Christ and those scars
His permanent scars
That brought permanent comfort to all those who believe in Him

Amen!

Story Behind the Poem

I read the book of James while on vacation in Florida. The main reason was to get temporary relief from the long winter we experienced in 2013/2014. There was snow at my house for more than six months and temperatures were colder than normal. I longed for the simple ability to walk out of a store and have the weather be comfortable. I wanted to be able to wear shorts, a short-sleeved shirt, or hooded sweatshirt and be comfortable. When we arrived in Florida, the weather matched my first desire although it was overcast and cloudy. I desired sunshine and warmer temperatures.

The statement about obedience came from a saying that the place with the most obedience is Hell because that is all residents have. They don't have the peace or comfort God offers to all who accept Christ as their Lord and Savior. The world is one distraction after another. I never feel quite comfortable in anything I do anymore, and I long for Heaven!

Poem 21 – Conceal

Scripture: Luke 8:17, 1 John 4:8, James 4:3

Poem

I will let my family down
I will let my employer down
I will let the world down
If I try to conceal a problem
Scripture states, all things will be brought into light
Nothing will be able to hide
There are many unknowns in life's journey
Ask God for help along the way
When we ask for guidance with pure thoughts
Our prayers will be answered
If there is anything we try to hide from Him
Absolutely everything will be revealed
Every word, every action, every deed
When we realize everything will be judged
We need to accept Jesus as our Savior
One small thing can stand in the way of doing that -- pride
Pride has been said to be the root of all sin
Pride breeds distraction, doubt
When we have distractions
It interferes with hearing God's small, still voice
God prompts in simple ways
He gives us direction differently for each person
When we long to please Him
He likes this and it's called worship
We should not be surprised when we fail
The enemy is along for the ride
When our emotions are down

The enemy helps reinforce failure
We are reminded of our failures, doubts, and half-truths
This casts doubt on our ability to love God
We are not worthy of His love
God will gently remind us He's there
He hasn't forgotten His sheep
He will venture away from the flock to save just one
All of us on the path to Heaven will have failures
How we react, how we respond, and how we seek help is the key
Do we give up and wander away?
Or do we cling to God more than ever?
God will not forsake, He will not let go
Even though we fail, we try to conceal
Thank you God for your mercy and grace

Amen!

Story Behind the Poem

In my Christian walk, more challenges seem to happen the longer I walk with Him. Although my Bible knowledge and application of Scripture continues to grow, there are times I stumble (i.e. Say something that isn't nice, watch an inappropriate movie). Everyone will have failures. The way we respond is more important.

I keep feeling this prompt to do daily devotionals with my family. I wasn't quite sure how to start and ignored this prompt. While on vacation in Florida, we came across the *Duck Dynasty* devotional book. My wife purchased the book when we returned from our vacation, we used it occasionally for our devotionals.

God is always faithful and answers prayer when done appropriately, which is discussed in the book of James. The important thing mankind forgets the answer to prayer might not match the result we want: cure of a disease, a new job, correct answer to an everyday problem. All our actions, words, and deeds will be judged by God in the end. A clear conscience is a cherished thing we should strive for no matter the circumstance. If I try to conceal something, my conscience isn't clear.

Poem 22 – Chips

Scripture : Matthew 11:30, John 16:33, Jeremiah 31:3, Proverbs 17: 17

Poem

In the face of adversity
The chips are down
Everything around you is falling apart
Nothing, I mean nothing, is going right
The harder you try to fix things
The more broken your world becomes
You become frustrated to the point of no return
You wonder if the sorrow will ever end
You beg God for direction
His voice is silent at that very moment
You lean on your old habits
That have saved you in the past
They don't save you this time
You wonder, pray, and beg for relief
God has a plan. Right?!
I'm not sure what to do
At this moment in your life
You do not have control
Nor did you ever have control
Until you felt helpless
God asks, "Have you had enough yet?"
Are you ready to give it all to me?
In your human weakness, you hold back
You are too prideful to give up everything
We fall on our faces
We stumble to our knees

His gentle hand catches us ever so slightly
We do not realize He catches us until later in the journey
These moments could last for days or months
When we reach our lowest point
We hear His small still voice, had enough yet?
After many attempts and many failures
Bible verses seem to make more sense
Even though we might not understand completely
It becomes clear His word is the right path
We take each day as a gift
To those with limited time on this planet
Little things wither away, they enjoy the simple things
A visit from a friend
A conversation with a family member
What used to be boring is now interesting
They no longer try to control things
As His word says, my yoke is light
Don't worry, I've conquered the world
When we finally comprehend those simple statements
We can finally have true peace
Even when the chips are stacked against us
That small still voice says, I love you and you are mine!
Eternal love by our Heavenly father
Nothing can describe it!

Amen!

Story Behind the Poem

A couple things inspired this poem. 1) I was reading Scott Rigsby's story about losing his legs and having a traumatic brain injury. Some of his struggles, like saying what was on his mind, were difficult. It was an inspiration how his faith was involved in his journey to become an Ironman. 2) The theme of this book talks about my dad's struggle with cancer and my mom's emotions supporting him through the cancer treatments. The bills as well as the many days and weeks waiting for answers and direction are overwhelming.

For anyone who has been through a life-altering event, my thoughts and prayers go to them. I think the only person who can relate is Jesus, whose dying on the cross for us exceeds all forms of physical and mental pain. He can relate! I didn't realize I typed that and why this poem is called "Chips." In America, we have a saying, "When the chips are down," which means when things in life are not going your way. Somehow you'll find a way to succeed. I hope this story inspires you to seek God's wisdom and lean on Him, especially in times of struggle.

Poem 23 – Chuck

Scripture : Jeremiah 29:11

Poem

Do you have someone you can ask for advice?
You are not sure what to do at times
God provides people in our lives who know
Some would call them "Saints"
No matter the situation
They are calm and collected
They probably would tell you otherwise
When you ask them tough questions, they sit and ponder for a moment
They wait for a period of time before responding
When they do reply, they seem to speak the right words
When compassion is needed
They are there
When advice is needed
They give just the right direction
When leadership is needed
They step up and accept the challenge
God puts people like this in your life at the right moment
You know it when you meet them
God has a plan for all of his children
When we stumble, we have people there
Giving the right words of comfort
Giving direction to help through a difficult task
God thought of these individuals before they were born
God takes the bad and turns it to good
He uses good people in the most difficult times
Whether the advice is something simple or life-altering

The most knowledgeable people are the most humble
They realize they are not in control, God is
They do NOT lean on their own understanding
I wish I had these traits, maybe someday
Maybe God is grooming us to be like Chuck one day
Until then, I'm glad God gave us people like this
Patient, knowledgeable, talented in so many ways
Yet humble enough to give God all the glory
He was there at the right time
To provide the right answers and advice
God, you are awesome beyond words
Thank you for providing people like Chuck in our lives

Amen!

Story Behind the Poem

When I was first introduced to the concept of this book, I talked to Pastor Chuck Davenport. I told him that God laid the theme *"About the Letter C"* on my heart. I challenged him to find "C" words that were positive and reflected spiritual value. Pastor Chuck calmly thought for a moment, went to his laptop, and located a website with thousands of words that start with the letter C. Chuck, myself and a few others spent time discussing a few dozen words. The website just provided a spark, the wisdom and demeanor of Chuck was helpful defining a set of words to write poems about. I didn't use all the "C" words we talked about. The list of all "C" words we discussed are listed in the back of the book.

Pastor Chuck and his wife Marsha are in charge of the compassion ministry at my church. Chuck is a counselor and ordained pastor. His demeanor is calm yet concerned enough to want to help. His personality is genuine and caring and he wants to do the right thing. After writing the poem called "Chips," which is the previous story in the book, I realized when the "Chips" are down, we need people like Chuck in our lives. I'm thankful for people like Pastor Chuck, when the "Chips" are down and we face adversity, they are willing to provide direction.

Poem 24 – Curb

Scripture : Ecclesiastes 10:10, Proverbs 27:27, John 18:1-11

Poem

You are driving down the street
Nothing out of the ordinary is happening
You are observing life and surroundings God provides
Thinking of nothing important
You are in a fog
You drift your vehicle ever so slightly and bump the curb
Instantly, you pull the steering wheel back correcting your position
You are shaken and notice others observed you hitting the curb
Your confidence is shaken, your heart is racing
Your palms are sweating
You become defensive
Negative thoughts race through mind
You keep thinking, how can that happen to me?
I'm a good driver, you become prideful
Over and over the negative thoughts gets bigger
The curb abruptly corrects you, no grace, no mercy
Events in life get in the way of focusing on Jesus Christ
The Holy Ghost will nudge you
Reminding you like the curb, unlike cement curbs
God's curb will direct you in the right direction
He reminds you of His son Jesus
His ministry was a short three years
It would end abruptly like hitting the curb
Along the way, He corrected many
Some listened, some didn't

In the end, like the curb
If we don't correct our thoughts and actions
We will experience an eternal separation from our Savior
Thank you, Jesus, for putting curbs in our lives to help correct us
This helps keep us straight and focused on you!

Amen!

Story Behind the Poem

I've bumped curbs while driving, they abruptly let you know the car has wandered too far off course. The word curb was a good description of helping redirect a car when it wanders too far off the road. As in life, we need correction every so often.

Secondly, I was driving to work and feeling like I just woke up. At a busy corner waiting to turn left, I thought to go but didn't. It's a good thing I didn't because I would have turned in front of a car. It scared me a lot. I thank God that very moment for not having me push the gas pedal.

Occasionally, we need curbs (aka reminders) in our lives to direct our efforts back to Jesus.

Poem 25 – Characterize

Scripture : Proverbs 10

Poem

You come home one day from work
A simple question from a loved one catches you off guard
Earlier in life, you would have said no big deal
As you get older, you think more before answering
People assume you answer yes, without saying yes verbally
The conversation ends
You ponder the decision you made
You ask God honestly, what are you doing?
The more you think about your decision
The more you get frustrated
You feel a twinge in your left shoulder
This indicates stress
You question God
The question your family asked tests your integrity
You have a choice, be deceptive or not
Every one you talk to says it'll be ok
This provides a perspective from other people
The initial decision does not make your conscience feel good
Your loved ones won't understand
They wonder why I'm over-thinking the decision
It won't hurt anyone
We will get what we want
You discuss this further with your spouse, there is a disagreement
They say don't go to bed angry
This is in Scripture
I ignored the advice

I didn't sleep very well
After praying and thinking
I choose integrity over what other people said was okay
My decision is not the easy way out, just like our Savior did
Jesus chose the right way
Showed us how to have integrity
The story has yet to complete
Much like our walk on this Earth
Until faith becomes sight
Integrity is the only thing we have in tough times
Thanks Jesus for displaying how to act
Making decisions from a kingdom perspective

Amen!

Story Behind the Poem

I was asked one day to do something that went against my better judgment. My first response was not to answer. The assumption was I would answer yes. The more I thought about it, the more I realized my integrity would be tested. I pondered and couldn't give in although my spouse and I wouldn't agree on the answer. The decision would cost us a few hundred dollars we wouldn't get back.

I went to bed angry although Scripture says to not let the sun go down while angry (Ephesians 4:26). Against that better advice, I didn't sleep much that night. I prayed and thought, 'What can I do to keep from spending money and keep my wife happy?'

If I chose to keep my spouse happy, my conscience would not be clear. In the end, I typed a response to my wife explaining my thoughts. It came down to integrity. Just like Jesus in a way, He could have commanded Heaven's armies to save him, he chose not to while suffering on the Cross. My character is worth more than a few hundred dollars. In my experience, the Lord will replace it one day. How would you characterize your integrity in a tough situation?

Poem 26 – Curse

Scripture : Jeremiah 29:11-13

Poem

Is something a burden?
It makes you wonder why it has to be so hard
Days, months go by, the same burden
You wonder, will it ever go away
You ask God, why me? Why this?
I wonder to myself why God would give me such a thing
Deep down, we never think about the opposite
Is this curse a blessing?
A blessing that causes so much pain
Months go by, similar pain, things happen in a rhythm
God has provided this blessing to many people
It takes certain people to handle this blessing
Many would fail if they had to carry this burden
A blessing from God is special
It takes many shapes and sizes
The blessing will mold us, change us from the inside out
There are days we ask God to give this blessing to someone else
It causes discomfort, headaches, and weight gain
Jesus bore the ultimate pain
He died on the cross, bore all sin for all time
Stop and think for a second
He had the ultimate comfort
He had eternal peace, was a king in Heaven
He accepted the burden, which was a blessing for everyone
Not just everyone of his day
Everyone for all time

When you question God's intention
You are putting yourself at the same level as God
Think about His design, His greater purpose
He is much more interested in what you will become
Than how you are currently
He has plans for you and for others by what you do
Some may wonder, many will question
The answer might not be known until we reach Heaven
The next time you wonder, the next time you ask
Seek Him in his Word, and seek Him in prayer
Ask Him to use you for His ultimate plan
Even if we don't know what the burden will be
There is a blessing at the end of the journey
Those who seek Him will realize their burdens will have paid off
It's only a curse when you are distracted from God
When we accept His will, it's a true blessing

Amen!

Story Behind the Poem

This story was originally designed to explain in detail differences between a man and woman God has inspired. God placed man over his wife as God is over man. A woman's place is to support the household, have children, and be a supporter. There are monthly challenges placed on a woman during her childbearing years that involve discomfort, headaches, and more. Many refer to this as the "curse."
This implementation by God is a blessing to provide life. It's unique and original and there is nothing else like it. Mankind can try to recreate things, but the actual technique, its design, how it's planned, and the entire process is designed by God alone. Every life is blessed by God and is a true miracle.

Sometimes in life, God will seem to put one mountain in front of another. We wonder, we doubt, and just get annoyed. When we are frustrated, the thought of a blessing is far from our thoughts. All we are concerned about at the time is discomfort, feeling tired, this ache or that ache. The book is titled *33: About the Letter C*. It includes many stories about people and their "big C." I can only imagine the challenges, questions, and pain involved in their journeys. I won't confess I understand what they went through. In comparison, just like writing devotional books, I wonder sometimes if it's a curse or a blessing.

I don't know the outcome, whom it will affect, how it impacts their lives. For someone who is task-oriented and likes to know the impact of his efforts, the unknown seems like a curse. I write many of the stories in the early morning hours, which causes me to lose sleep. Some would appreciate the quiet, joyful, and inspiring time the Holy Spirit takes over and writes God-inspired poems. It's not a curse but a true blessing. Here is a prayer God inspired in me while I wrote this story for those who need help with perspective in a difficult situation.

"Heavenly Father, you are the creator of all things. You have the ultimate plan no one else can understand. I am more concerned with the here and now than what will happen in the future. The unknown is hard to take; we seek your wisdom, and we seek your knowledge. Please use this situation to help me grow to further your kingdom, witness to everyone who will listen.

"Many today reject you, many doubt your existence, and ultimately challenge your authority. They forget or don't want to acknowledge your eternal power. More importantly, they ignore your love, grace, and mercy. Someday these people could be in the same situation but will fight a perceived curse alone without your comforting words and knowing the blessing Jesus provided for us."

"Lord, I hand over these aches, pains, and doubt to you. Please provide me physical comfort and peace of mind enough to make it through this day, so I may have another day to share my story so it may bless others to see their lives as a blessing and not a curse"

Poem 27 – Cure

Scripture : Luke 2:1-20

Poem

We go about our daily routine without thinking
We take small things for granted
One day, out of nowhere, something happens
Something not normal is noticed
A twinge, a short pain, a growth
We wonder what it is
We go to the doctor or health specialist
More tests are run than a person thought possible
The results come back, its positive
Something is mutating in your body
It's not normal, it's destroying things
If left unchecked, it can take your life
All the normal, pleasant, unassuming things are gone
You ask yourself, why me, what's next?
Some may wonder what is God thinking
Me, little ole' me and how can God benefit from this
You pray for a cure, you pray for healing
This can take many shapes and paths
The cure for most involves putting poison into your body
Then a dose of radiation
Like something cooked in the microwave
This is intended to kill off or stop the growth
Some cures involve surgery that has its own battles
Healing after surgery is not easy, regardless how small the procedure
Take the mental challenges that go with this battle
Not going to war in the normal sense

You are in a battle nonetheless
Every moment of every day
The very essence of this disease is like the enemy
It lurks, hangs around, then starts to grow
If left unchecked, it takes over your life
It will eventually take over and can cause spiritual death
What can become of a life-altering change such as this?
To whom can we turn for comfort and healing
There are doctors, nurses, specialists with lots of knowledge and training
God blessed them with a gift to save what is most precious, life
For both mental and physical aspects
Turning to God provides more blessings than one can describe
In one sense, the impact makes one question God
In the other, we hand everything over to him
We want that sense of normalcy back
Where we can assume things are normal
We are all on this Earth temporarily
Our journey is short, all have challenges
When we or a loved one is handed a health issue
It's one more way we'll appreciate when we see Jesus
Some might be angry at God
Some might not want His blessing, grace, and mercy
It's a choice we have even in tough times
God is patient, kind, and waiting for our attention
God provided His son Jesus Christ as our Savior
He is the cure for eternal life
For some, it takes a life-altering event
To wake up and take notice
Our hope and prayer for a cure is in God's hands
He handed us a spiritual cure through his son Jesus
Regardless of what we face on Earth
God is there, loving, caring even though we may question
Put your hope and faith in Him

In the end, your eternity rests on a simple choice
Choose bitterness, hate, and regret
Or choose love, forgiveness, and reflection
I chose the latter, I chose Jesus Christ
As my cure for eternal salvation.

Amen!

Story Behind the Poem

I was hearing a sermon about 1 Corinthians. I forget the details although, during the sermon outline, the word cure was displayed. I felt God mention, 'Here is another "C" word.' What would it be like to hear from a doctor, "You have a disease." And also in the same journey, you hear, "You are cured." Words can't describe the situation I imagine. Many have praised God for healing and, once healed, praise him more.

His heart must fill with happiness when we show such joy and love. He wants our undivided attention. He wants to be first in our lives. We praise, interact through many forms of worship. This is what we are designed for. When sin entered the world, it destroyed things in ways no one can describe. Through His son Jesus Christ, we have a spiritual cure. The term "spiritual cure" appeared when I was writing this story. I've ask others to share their stories about how cancer impacted their lives. I'm humbled to have God lead me on the journey writing 33. My hope is the poems, stories, and resources supplied help others.

I wonder if hearing from others provides hope in their struggle? A cure can take shape by knowing where to get assistance, help, or information. I won't even begin to understand the struggle, battle to fight this disease.
My hope people accept Jesus in their hearts knowing, regardless of the outcome for themselves or a loved one, they'll return to Jesus. Jesus provided a cure 2,000+ years ago. He suffered greatly, endured indescribable pain for our eternal lives. That might not seem like a cure, but the other choice is to be separated from Him and our heavenly Father.

No matter what happens on Earth, this simple, free gift is the best cure one can have. Continue to fight, battle, pray, and share your story while you can. It can impact others in ways that can't be measured in this lifetime. We all seek a cure, and that will take many shapes and forms. Regardless of that, please, please accept Jesus as your Savior!

Poem 28 – Connection

Scripture : 1 Timothy 6:12-16, Acts 19:40

Poem

A connection is two things joining together
A power cord plugged into an outlet
A light bulb and a socket
Your hand in a baseball glove
It can also be a hammer and a nail
An ax splitting wood
A child hugging his mother or father
A man and women getting married
We tend to be busy as humans
We go about our days doing things
Going from one activity to another
Not thinking too far into the future
For we don't know how many days we have
Nor do we stop to think when things are going along
We take our days and nights for granted
The good Lord has nature in a rhythm
Our lives connect in certain ways to this pattern
We don't stop to think about it much
Something happens in our lives
An event of some sort that makes us think
If this person moves away or is gone
What will happen, how will it impact our connection
Time with people is short
Earlier in life, things just happen
You take it for granted they'll be around forever
Then one day a child grows up
A parent or grandparent grows old

They depart either by moving or passing on
Each connection is unique and serves a purpose
A spiritual connection is different
Unlike examples mentioned above
This can't be easily seen
When we accept Christ, a spiritual connection happens
It's the most important connection we can make on earth
God wants all His children to make a connection with Him
He loved us so much, He gave us free will
We get to choose if a connection is made with Him
The connection with God is the most important
Cherish your earthly connections
Enjoy every moment, every opportunity to connect
They could change at any moment
The connection with God is eternal
We were made to have a relationship with Him
Even in our fallen world, God made a way
Do you know of someone who hasn't connected to God lately?
Pray for this person, tell him or her about your connection to the Father
One day in Heaven, this person will thank you
He or she will be eternally grateful

Amen!

Story Behind the Poem

For those with children, a connection or bond is made that can't be explained except for "It's there." One moment they are growing up, barely able to care for themselves. The next moment they are entering school, the next they are as tall as you are, they get their driver's license. When they leave home for short trips, the connection you made when they were young can be broken if something happens.

I experienced this fear when my youngest son got his driver's license. It made me realize my oldest was overseas serving our country and my middle son moved out and bought his own home. The connections made were changing before my very eyes. Along with this life change, my father has been battling cancer.

The connection I had with my dad was special. I respected him and thought there was no person better when I was a kid. He owned his own business and could do practically anything. There was nothing too big for him. He was my idol as a kid. I was proud he was my dad. Every time I did something exciting, I wanted to tell him. His encouraging words made a connection, a positive one that helped complete whatever I was doing at the time.

My connection with God has been similar. As I write this story, it brings me to tears to my eyes. Special connections should be enjoyed. A relationship with God is eternal. Please be sure to tell everyone about your relationship with God. If you are reading this and don't know God, ask someone you know who is spiritual and believes in God. The moral of this story is to enjoy whatever connections you have with special people, the relationship could change in an instant.

Poem 29 – Celebrate

Scripture : Ephesians 4:11 to 4:13

Poem

When we celebrate moments in life
We should be humble and appreciate small things
There are times of great triumph in life
We celebrate these victories with many people
Sporting events are among those times
When our favorite team wins, we feel good
When our favorite people do well
We enjoy the moment of success
When we fall short, we ponder
We long for the days of success
Youth is much like that
When we are young
We want to be older
We want something else
As we get older
Some long for days of youth
We never seem to stop long enough to celebrate
There are short times of enjoyment
Regardless of the situation
Regardless of the time
We should celebrate the best we can
Celebrate with every ounce of our being
God will come alongside us
We should give thanks no matter what is happening
Things will happen in life
Some are small, some are big
They will challenge us greatly

We wonder where our energy will come from
God will be there through all situations
We should stop, take a breath, and realize ourselves in the moment
The enemy will get try to get us thinking about the bad things
His distractions will abound, his attacks will happen often
Days turns into weeks
Weeks into months
When we stop and think
We have forgotten about Jesus
This is the goal of the enemy
The more we are distracted
The less we are focused on the Kingdom
In all of this, God is still there
He still loves us
With eternal patience waiting for us
When we stop and realize what the enemy is doing
We ask for forgiveness, God and his angels celebrate
They rejoice in Heaven
It's not something we yet understand
Until that day is realized, we have faith
We should celebrate our faith
No matter what is happening in your life
God already knows what will happen
He just wants our hearts
When we accept Jesus, we can celebrate
Until the end
We should try to be thankful
To celebrate and share our relationship with Jesus
After all, it's our choice
To focus on Him or ourselves
Jesus wants us to focus on Him
God is big and so are His celebrations
We can't begin to understand the day when His son returns
Until then, celebrate all things

Whatever it is, thank God
In one day, our faith will become sight
That day, we celebrate more than we can understand

Amen!

Story Behind the Poem

This story talks about Marv and Tarry Everingham's journey with Marv's cancer. The story Tarry wrote is in the back of the book. Marv went through many battles while getting treatment that affected him physically, including his lifelong enjoyment of hunting and fishing. His eye sight was impacted as well, and he often wore sunglasses.

Tarry documented how they leaned on their faith in Jesus during the battle. Marv was victorious in the battle and was cancer-free although the negative effects on his body were great. When I learned about Marv's passing, the first word that came to my mind was celebrate. His faith and battle became sight when he got to see Jesus and celebrate eternally in His kingdom.

While writing this story, I learned a 22-year-old man had died in a motorcycle accident. The story reinforced that we don't know how many days we have on this Earth, so we should celebrate each one as much as we can.

Our pastor stated God and His joy are large. Can you just imagine He has the power to create our universe? Imagine how He and His angels celebrate. It's beyond our comprehension.

Poem 30 – Compass

Scripture : Luke 6:41

Poem

What is your direction in life?
Up, down, sideways, or all of them?
Do you focus on everyday distractions?
Do they take your attention away from the Cross?
The more distractions you have
The more the enemy tries to cloud your faith
When change happens, opportunities arise
Depending on your focus, if you allow God to guide you
He can set your compass correctly
He can set your life straight and point toward His son
Even when things are going well
We can easily be thrown into confusion
The timing is never right
We take one wrong step
When our compass is not fully pointed toward Jesus
We need to work harder focusing on the Cross
It's easy to let the culture impact our lives
It only takes a single glance, a difficult situation to slip
This can impact others' walks with Jesus as well
They might be thrown off the road to salvation
When the Holy Spirit prompts
We need to heed His prompts
Don't allow distractions to impact your compass
The more distractions, the more we need to pray
Don't practice prayer, get in the game
PRAY, ask God to examine your heart
Make sure you turn over all things to God

Good, bad, or indifferent
God wants to be involved in your life
He loves us more than we will ever realize
When you notice your compass is broken
Make sure you don't have a plank in your eye
Before you judge others and think your faith is stronger
Take an inventory of your own compass
When we focus more on Jesus
The less we focus on ourselves
It keeps our compass pointed in the right direction
Towards Heaven and
Our eternal home, where all things are pointed

Amen!

Story Behind the Poem

Our church was covering 1 Corinthians, and it challenged me and the church. I was getting used to owning a camper and boat, which caused distraction in my life. Adult toys bring problems that require fixing. That caused frustration and it impacted my faith and took away from having my priorities right.

I was doing my devotionals, asking God what the remaining words for this book should be when I noticed the car ahead was a Toyota Compass. I had five stories to finish. The Holy Spirit prompted me with celebrate, compass, chemo, cross, and Christ or potentially caregiver. Cross was eventually wrapped into the Christ poem and I wrote ""Caregiver" (number 32 poem)

SECTION 3 – His Ministry Begins, Changes World Forever

Jesus began his ministry when He was about 30 (Luke 3:23). Until then, other than a brief mention when Jesus was 12, God did not reveal details. When Jesus started his ministry, He began with miracles and turned water into wine.

Here is another amazing testimony by Shavonne Smith that shows the power and grace God provides in times of need, especially when we lean on Him for everything.

Shavonne Smith's Testimony

Have you ever heard that Francesca Battistelli song, "Write Your Story"? There is a that says, "I want my history, to be a legacy, go ahead and show this world, what you've done in me."

My story begins when I was about two years old. My mom had a nervous breakdown. That night, my dad got on his knees, (one of the first times ever for him) and really prayed to the Lord. He asked God to heal my mom and said, "If you heal her, I will commit my life to you and start going to church." Well, the very next day my mom began to recover. A nurse ministered to Mom, prayed with her to receive Jesus, and encouraged her to start going to church. So Mom and I began attending church. Dad still wasn't ready at that time. I hear stories that we prayed nightly for five years, and then he started coming and committed his life to the Lord too.

Time went by and when I was in middle school, a quarter-sized bald spot appeared on the back of my head. My parents took me to a dermatologist who did a biopsy on the spot. The test results showed the spot needed to be removed. At that time, my parents had been faithfully watching The 700 Club. If you have watched this show, you know many miracles happen when Pat Robertson prays.

My parents sat me down, got out the vegetable oil, and read James 5:14 and 15 to me. They said, "Okay, we are going to pray and anoint you with oil and believe for your healing." I said, Okay." About a month later, I had an appointment in Lansing to have the spot removed. We drove there but the surgeon could not find the bald spot.

The doctor, who did the biopsy, finally found the small scar where he had done the biopsy. The hair had already started to grow back and was a few inches long, in the spot that had been bald. The doctors just shook their heads and said we could go. I cried for happiness! Having your head shaved was the worst possible thought for a middle school age person. I told the doctor right away that Jesus had healed me! I knew He had.

A year or two later, we started going to a Bible study at my parents' friend's house. Every week they held the study with prayer at the end. Each week we dug deeper into the Word of God and learned. Going to church on Sunday is great, but you need more than that to live a successful Christian life and not just a Christian life.

God did many amazing miracles for me during my high school years. I remember one particular morning, I had made a bad mistake the night before and felt horrible. I asked God if He could see fit to forgive me again. The sun came out from behind a cloud and started to shine on me. The Lord spoke to me and said, "It's a new day." Isn't God so good? This is my favorite high school miracle.

One night, I went to Bible study when I had mono. I went into the bathroom before study time, opened my mouth, and looked in my throat, which was covered in white spots. During prayer time after study was over, everyone laid hands on me and prayed for my healing. The pain was gone instantly. I went back into the bathroom and checked my throat again. The white spots were gone! Jesus not only forgives our sins, but He heals all our diseases!

More time goes by, I found my husband God has planned for me, and we got married in 1995. We decide to start a family in 1996. Several miscarriages and one tubal pregnancy later, fast forward to March 2003. I heard from a friend about a book called Supernatural Childbirth by Jackie Mize. I read the book and listened to the tape until I had it memorized! Amazing encouragement for a woman waiting for a child.

One Sunday in March, five months after having a tubal pregnancy, I went to church with my husband. I am normally a very positive person, but for the first time in my life depression was trying to overtake me. I could not lift my hands in worship, which has never happened, so I cried out to the Lord. "Please take this depression from me, Lord I cannot deal with feeling this way. I know it is your will that we have a child and you know how badly I want one Lord.

Driving home from church, we passed a car dealership that had my favorite car in my favorite color on display, it was a bright blue BMW Z3 convertible. We looked at that car and my husband said, "Shavonne, if you go get your tubes tied, I will buy you that car." My husband was serious. He was tired of all we had gone through as well and had decided we could have things instead. I remember turning to him and responding, "No. Let's just try one more time." Depression left me instantly.

A week or so later, a friend I worked with pushed me into our breakroom on the last day I could sign up for medical insurance. She told me to get insurance and make an appointment with her doctor, a fertility specialist and a Christian. Nothing is a coincidence with God. I became pregnant with our daughter.

The following month, the doctor prescribed with a drug that would help me keep this baby. The drug also made me very sick to my stomach. I recall being in the breakroom at work and being sick frequently. At that time, I worked with a girl who was a compulsive liar. I have no other way to describe her -- she had issues. I went home sick another day, and she thought it would be fun to stir up drama and tell my co-workers I was going home because I was miscarrying again.

I was at home when a friend from work called me to tell me the news. Boy was I angry! I took it to the Lord and decided the best way to deal with her was to confront her. Because she lied so much, I took her and my manager into the breakroom, and I told her, "I did not go home bleeding. I am not going to miscarry again. You may not speak anything negative about my baby, about me or my husband or family ever again."

This was a HUGE blessing in disguise because WORDS are so powerful. When you dig deep into your Bible, you can see that God created with His words. Jesus healed with His words. Jesus killed the fig tree with His words. Proverbs 18:21 (NASB) "Death and life are in the power of the tongue, And those who love it will eat its fruit." Mark 11:23 (NASB) " Truly I say to you, whoever says to this mountain, 'Be taken up and cast into the sea,' and does not doubt in his heart, but believes that what he says is going to happen, it will be granted him." I was proclaiming the truth over my body and my situation and didn't realize at the time how powerful my words were!

Our miracle girl was born in January 2004. In December 2005, I lost the best friend I will ever have to breast cancer – my mother. What an incredible woman of God she was. I miss her terribly and look forward to the day I will see her again. Three days after Mom's funeral (Don't ask me why three days but I remember it so clearly!) I awoke in the morning and realized, "Who is going to pray for me now? Who will pray for my family members? Who will stand in faith with me for miracles to happen?" It hit me like a train. She was gone.

Who else would take up this mantle? I knew the answer. I knew I had to change my ways now. No more just going to church every Sunday and Bible studies to get all I needed from the Lord. No more praying only once in a while when I needed something. Life changed so I changed. My prayer life began. Several miracles and 10 years later is when my C story begins. January 2014.

My husband and I noticed a lump in my breast. Of course we prayed for negative mammogram results. The test came back negative. February came AND I kept feeling that Rich AND I needed to get a family doctor for both of us. We lived here eight years, SO IT WAS about time to get one. We went for exams for first-time patients, and the doctor did not like the way the lump looked and felt, so she sent me to Grand Rapids.

In March, I saw a doctor in Grand Rapids. She did not like the way the lump looked on the ultrasound did a biopsy then and there. Three days later, the nurse called to tell me the results were positive, the lump was indeed the big C. Amazing thing, they knew what it was caused from! It was a kind of drug a doctor had me take, years ago. Amazing technology these days.

Out of fear and remembering all my mother had gone through, I told the doctor if the tests were positive, I wanted everything removed. Can anyone tell me after reading my whole story what I did wrong there? I spoke out of fear! I should have kept my negative mouth closed! I called my best friend, and she advised me to have someone close to me pray over me and anoint me with oil like it says to do in James 5:14.

Rich and I went to the church we were married in and had our pastor, his wife, and two elders meet with us and pray over me. From the moment I left after they prayed for me, I felt like I was enveloped in a blanket of peace that carried me almost all the way to my surgery day. We had prayed and agreed that I would recover quickly, that they would not find cancer in my lymph nodes, and that I would not need radiation or chemotherapy. (My doctor informed me they test the nodes during the surgery.)

Genetic testing came before surgery. A funny thing happened in the conference room at genetic testing. They asked me point blank if I thought the test would be positive because my grandfather (Mom's dad), and Mom had both died from breast cancer. I said, "No, I do not believe it will be positive. We've each had cancer for different reasons."

Satan enjoyed playing with my thoughts during the waiting time for those test results. Satan is a thief and a liar and all he wants to do is to steal from you, kill you, and destroy your family. I was attacked by him like never before during March and April. He woke me night after night and harassed me with horrible thoughts. When he does that to you, you need to speak aloud James 4:7 (NASB), "Submit yourselves therefore to God, resist the devil, and he WILL flee from you." Say it over and over if you have to. 2 Timothy 1:7 "For God has not given us a spirit of timidity, but of power and love and discipline."

A few days before the surgery was scheduled, a nurse called to tell me when I could eat and drink. At the end of our conversation, she said, "So you are having a double mastectomy and having expanders placed by the plastic surgeon." "And having my ovaries removed," I said. She replied, "I don't have that written down here." I had asked my doctor if I could have everything done at the same time. We miscommunicated, which meant I was going to have another surgery before what was to have been the first surgery.

I was completely thrown out of peace and into full panic mode! I called every doctor I knew and none could remove my ovaries on Monday at the time of the surgery. My doctor told me the type of cancer in my body was fueled by hormones, so I needed to have my ovaries removed or stop my monthlies from coming.

I was panicking and wanting to get these things out as soon as possible! That didn't happen and I had the double mastectomy on April 14, Passover Eve. I also had the most incredible Christian nurse she attended my every need and helped me above and beyond on the hardest night of my life. I mention her because God answers all your prayers specifically, and a friend had prayed for a great nurse for me.

A few days after my surgery, I received a horrible phone call telling me I would need another surgery. They had found cancer in another node following surgery, when they looked at one node closer! I was in shock. I thought to myself, 'But God, I asked you specifically for all these things, and you answered every single time before. Why is this happening?'

The Lord told me to read James. I read there that if I asked for wisdom from the Lord, He WOULD give it to me.
I asked for wisdom and I began seeking the Lord like never before in my life you have un-forgiveness against anyone for any reason, I read, you better take care of it or your prayers won't be answered! I thought about that and took care of all the apologies I felt the Lord wanted me to. I already knew from other times in my life that God wanted to heal me. I was perplexed about why I kept asking for things and He would answer but not in the way I wanted.

Another surgery was scheduled for May 2 to have more lymph nodes removed. This is when I started to seek the Lord like never before in my life. I had prayed and God had answered many times, but healing was a scary subject for me. I had believed in healing for my mom too, remember. I had asked and asked, but it did not happen for her.

Exactly nine days before my second surgery, my doctor said she could not find a doctor in Grand Rapids who could remove my ovaries at the same time as the lymph nodes, so I would need another surgery. You just have to laugh at this point. Seriously?!

I was getting stronger in my faith, so I was not as shaken this time. I remember the nurse saying, "You know, you will probably have to have radiation after you have these lymph nodes removed." I just looked at her and said inside, 'No I won't!!!' She asked, "Did you hear what I said?" I said, "Yes, I heard what you said." That's not what my God says. That's not what I say in agreement with my God!

My husband was my encourager, and told me exactly what I needed to hear. "Why are you so worked up about everything? God will take care of you, everything will work out fine even if you have to have another surgery."

Nine days before the second lymph node surgery, I met with my OBGYN. On our way to the office, we prayed God would give me favor with this doctor. I must have said it 100 times before the doctor came into the room, "God hath not given me the spirit of fear, but of power, of love and of a sound mind." The doctor's scheduler, who was one of the people I called in a panic and who said I couldn't have my ovaries removed until six weeks after the mastectomy, talked with me.

The scheduler was one of the people I called in a panic and she had told me that I told her why I needed to have my ovaries removed quickly and, because I trusted her, I told her I would go through a third surgery if I needed to. She responded, "That won't be necessary. Someone in Grand Rapids does surgery on Fridays, and I will get someone to take your ovaries out at the same time as your lymph nodes."

Two days later, I had an appointment to meet a new doctor in Grand Rapids. Remember that my other doctor had asked all the OBGYNs in Grand Rapids, and none was available. During the first visit with the new doctor, he told me he might have to cancel his last two appointments for that day, but he would make it to my surgery. Thank you Jesus! Another miracle! Now just because you were saved and you haven't seen God do miracles like I have means nothing to God. He loves all His children all the same. If you ask Him for wisdom and ask Him for healing, He will do the same for you.

May 2nd arrived, and Rich and I drove to the hospital. I played praise music on the way, but I wasn't feeling at peace about having a second surgery. The song "Worthy Is the Lamb" by Darlene Czech came on and as I was singing it with closed eyes, I saw Jesus kneeling, hunched over, taking the whipping for my healing, taking those stripes upon His back.

I began to cry and He said, "I took those stripes for you." I replied, "You didn't do that for nothing in my life, Jesus. "I receive my healing." I was overwhelmed. Right before surgery, He showed up before surgery to show me I didn't have to pray specific things and stand on words that I say" Healing is different," He said. "I paid that price for you already. All you have to do is receive it, just like salvation."

In August of 2013, we decided to visit Disneyworld for a week, our biggest family vacation so far, and we were to fly out May 11. Lymph node and ovary surgery were May 2. The nurse did not want to remove the drain from under my arm until a week later on May 9.

At that point, I KNEW I would be fine. I was so steeped in the word of God that it was flowing from my lips all day every day, and that day was no different. I told her, "I will sign something if you need me to, but I do not need this drain and I will be fine. I am healed!" I witnessed to her and encouraged her. She took the drain out and said, "I know you will be fine without this drain. Have a fun vacation!" And we did.

Sometime before the first surgery, the doctor gave me a huge book about having cancer. I began to read and discovered the whole book was filled with worst-case scenarios. It was horrible! I threw the book on the floor, and it's still there today. I need to burn it.

I was reminded that where you spend the most time is where your mind will dwell. Luke 6:45 "The good man out of the good treasure of his heart brings forth what is good; and the evil man out of the evil treasure brings forth what is evil; for his mouth speaks from that which fills his heart." Psalms 91:1 (NASB) He who dwells in the shelter of the Most High Will abide in the shadow of the Almighty."

I began instead to read a book titled You Can Be Healed by Billy Jo Daughtry. Simple book really but extremely powerful message inside. I began to read out loud daily all the Scriptures that pertain to healing at the end of that book.

I stopped playing on Facebook and stopped chatting on the phone to friends. Instead, I prayed, read, and listened to preaching online that pertained to healing. I was SEEKING the Lord, like never before because my life depended on it! Is your life worth the investment of time? Be diligent in your seeking the Lord and when you start putting all your focus on Him, Satan will whisper lies in your ear.

You will know it is not from the Lord because the Lord has GOOD plans for your life. You will be able to say instantly, "No! In the name of Jesus, He bore my sicknesses and carried my pains, and by His stripes, I am healed." Isaiah 53:4 and5.

My husband and I decided we would tell only a few people what was going on in my life. We did not want to hear negative words or have well-meaning people call daily to ask, "How are you today?" Don't get me wrong. You may think you need that kind of support, but I learned through this that the only support you truly need is in His Word. Jeremiah 29:11, God said, "For I know the plans I have for you, declares the Lord, plans to prosper you and not to harm you. Plans to give you hope and a future."

But everybody stops there!!! We don't like to read on in Jeremiah 29:12 & 13. "THEN you will call on me and come and pray to me, and I will listen to you. You will seek me and find me, when you seek me with all your heart, I will be found by you, declares the Lord." He promises you will find Him if you seek Him with all your heart. God is so good. All the time.

Poem 31 – Chemo

Scripture : Isaiah 53

Poem

It called chemotherapy
It's designed to help deal with a bad disease
It a process to break down the body's immune system
It brings the body to the brink of physical exhaustion, sometimes beyond
Emotionally, it's nothing like a person has experienced before
This is the first phase potentially preparing for radiation
Neither process is healthy
The alternative is potential certain death
According to mainstream medicine
It's the only way to treat such a disease
Sometimes a pill is taken
Sometimes a shot is given
Some require surgery, some do not
Other times all three are used
The side effects are many
Lost hair, weight, stamina to name a few
The desire to do anything is almost certainly lost
Sleep is deprived, energy is greatly impacted
The will to live is a basic instinct
Until we are pushed to the brink
We never know our true boundaries
Chemotherapy, which is designed to help
Tests all phases of our existence
Physical, mental, emotional, and spiritual
There is nothing left hidden
From the effects this disease can have

There are many forms of the disease
Some are more severe than others
Regardless of which one
They all have one goal, to destroy cells
Chemo, as it's referred to
Is meant to help overcome
Many times along the journey
Many, many questions arise
Why did I get this?
Why am I doing this to myself?
Will it really help in the end?
Will it make a difference?
These are all valid questions
To some we will never know the answers
Every person's experience is different
No two journeys are the same
There are similar things
There is bond for those who have made the journey
Some seek spiritual guidance
Some seek other forms of help
All are meant to help deal with physical and emotional pain
The ultimate goal is get back to normal
One path is to lean on God
Some will be angry at Him
Why did you allow this to happen to me?
It not only impacts me, but my family and friends too
The anger is one stage of dealing with blunt change
Acceptance can be a long, drawn out process, some never reach it
Not sure anyone ever accepts the limitations
They do the best they can with how they feel
Its one day at a time
Planning is a thing of the past
Depending on how the body is doing
Will determine what activities are attempted

Through all this trial and tribulation
One day we all will walk into eternity
With the experience chemo gives us
We will have more stories to share
God, we can't begin to understand why this is happening
All we can ask is use us for your cause
My prayer is simple:
"The words I say
The thoughts I have
The actions I do
All reflect back to you"
My hope is my experiences help others
My desire is to make a difference
Ultimately, it's up to our Creator
Who is sovereign and has a plan for us
It's up to us to accept or reject
We have the free will to choose our paths
Like chemo, many things in life are meant to help
Experiences will happen, some good, some not
We have to come to the realization
We will NEVER have all the answers
Regardless how much we want to
It's probably in God's grace we don't know all the answers
In our human form, we probably couldn't handle it
Maybe this is a true blessing from God
Only when we reach the other side
Will we know that answer
We probably won't care by then.

Amen!

Story Behind the Poem

My question to God is, "why am I writing about something I've never experienced firsthand?" From watching my father battle his cancer and advice from the doctor, don't let super glue hold you in your chair, go live the best you know how. Find a hobby, live to the fullest. Easy to say, hard to do.

Since my father's battles begin in March 2013, there have been many. Finishing one set of chemo and radiation treatments, waiting two months, and beginning again. Every two weeks, the big question to answer: "Is my white blood cell count high enough to receive more chemo?"

If it is, I get to feel bad for a few days, and sleep a lot. His recovery from chemo takes a few days and he gets back to somewhat normal. He can perform basic tasks although, over the longer term, the outcome is unknown. My prayers are often and humble asking God for quality of life, peace of mind and physical comfort from the impact of ongoing chemo.

Poem 32 – Caregiver

Scripture : Psalm 51:10-12, Proverbs 3:5-6, 1 Chronicles 28:20, 1 Peter 5:2-4, 1 Thessalonians 5:9-11

Poem

A loved one is impacted by a disease
After being diagnosed, they struggle
The person can no longer complete tasks they once did
There is a daily routine of dealing with their disease
Some days are better than others
Some are a real struggle
While the loved one is dealing with the disease
Another loved one stands by faithfully
Providing care, love, reassurance
They are on the front lines with their sick loved one
They provide care and encouragement
They also perform tasks once handled by the sick person
Every moment of every day
They are battling the disease too
It's not the same physically
Yet they struggle emotionally and spiritually to help
The feelings can be helplessness
The emotional toll adds up over time
The struggle impacts in ways others can see as well
Some become bitter, some regress, some become stronger
It's not easy being a caregiver
It's a calling that takes deep faith and persistence
We are not trained or usually prepared for tasks ahead
The questions, problems are not easily solved
We consult experts to help get our loved ones back to normal

Sometimes through grace things return to normal,
Sometimes not
We are forever changed
When bad news is given to our loved ones
Caregivers are impacted as well
Words can't express the helpless feeling
Extended family and friends are impacted too
Not the same as a caregiver
It's not easy to accept the challenge
We aren't given the choice when taking on the role of a caregiver
Humans don't like to be forced to do something
Something happened and we don't know why
During the struggle, bills, debt, and waiting
Hurry up and wait
The waiting can be days, weeks, or even months for answers
This takes a toll not only on the person who is sick
The caregiver is impacted as well
Emotions are like a rollercoaster
God provides direction in James 1:12 (NASB)
12 Blessed is a man who perseveres under trial;
for once he has been approved,
he will receive the crown of life which
the Lord has promised to those who love Him"
Saying these words from God is one thing
Living up to the words is another
During all the struggles
My hope is people pray and lean on God
That again is easier said than done
During the deepest struggles
We make choices on many things
Many of them are NOT easy to answer
Regardless of the journey
The service a caregiver provides is priceless
It's a God-given task

It's not for the weak at heart
May God provide wisdom, patience, mercy
May God show His awesome power during these times
Hand over all things to Him
Even in the beginning if you just say it
God, I give all things to you
I trust in your plan
We will be together for eternity
When we get to commune with the greatest caregiver, forever!

Amen!

Story Behind the Poem

Based on my father's cancer and reading others' testimonies, I see an absolute miracle in the loved ones who provide care. My mother would admit words can't describe aspects of the journey.

I will NOT even begin to say I understand because that would be an insult to those who have experienced the journey. Story 31 called "Chemo" is intended to provide a perspective of a person experiencing cancer, but "Caregiver" is from a perspective of people providing care.

While this can take many forms, being there is the biggest thing they can provide. Caregivers are not impacted the same physically, they are part of every doctor appointment, treatment, and emergency room visit. Emotionally, they battle the disease full-time while trying to live a normal life.

Depending on a person's age, their kids can be involved in the journey. As with some stories, the kids have the cancer and the parents are involved in the journey. Regardless of the situation, please realize the caregiver's role is not easy nor will it end. There is no escape, only brief stints during which a person gets relief from the burden.

During this battle, extended family is impacted as well. Sometimes we try to keep living a normal life yet we know better. All I know is the more we struggle, the more we should try not to handle it ourselves and give it to God. Words easily spoken and hard to act upon. All I ask for is, God, may you receive this prayer and provide grace, comfort to all caregivers.

Caregiver Prayer

"Heavenly father
You know all, you are sovereign
our plans are not understood by man
It's probably by your grace it's designed that way
We struggle as our loved ones struggle
We find joy when they find joy
We try to find peace when they are at peace
The daily struggles take a toll
Please provide them wisdom when wisdom is needed
Provide them comfort when comfort is needed
Provide them direction when decisions have to be made
Provide them helpers when help is needed
The burden is great
You are greater than the burden
During the journey, we lose focus on this
We are so busy dealing with everything
Remind us of your love, mercy and grace
These are obvious things, yet we can forget
Allow us to hand over all burdens
You are the ultimate healer and physician
If it's in your will
Provide the ability to return to normal
With a new sense of perspective and humility
To forget the little things
To have an eternal perspective
Focused on your son Jesus

Amen!

Poem 33 – Christ

Scripture : John 14:6

Poem

Christ Jesus is our Savior
He is our rock and our fortress
He did everything for us
He descended from Heaven to save us
He was holy and became human
Not everyone would do that, just one that I know of
For about 33 years He lived among us
About three years He preached
His words and examples will last forever
He loved us so much
His name is above all names
His actions speak for themselves
He died for us on a wooden Cross
He was sinless yet took on sin
He took on all sin for all people for all time
He bore this responsibility so we could be forgiven
Regardless of our struggle
Regardless of our situation
He's been there
He's done that
He is our Savior
He is our King
Thank you Jesus for being the example
Thank you for your love!

Amen!

Story Behind the Poem

Words don't do justice when describing what Jesus did for us. Every statement in the Bible I know of is clearly stated yet people debate what was said and even more what wasn't. For someone to be Holy and perfect, take on human flesh, and die the way He did for us is humbling. These words I'm writing can't even begin to say thank you.

As with every struggle described in this book, we don't know why. Frustration, anger, unknown, vague are a few adjectives describing the emotions. There is also physical pain, recovery from surgery, more diagnoses, more waiting than one can handle at times. Jesus understands these, and as we struggle and pray, He is there during our journey. Try to reflect on all situations. Sometimes it's easier, sometimes it's not.

I want to just say thank you, Jesus, for the challenge to write on such a difficult topic. For me, it's been most challenging and I'm just an outsider. My father and mother are the real heroes in the battle, and they wouldn't call themselves heroes. They would call it a battle.

Appendix

Jennifer Longfellow Family Story

I am trying to think of a word that can describe cancer, and I honestly cannot come up with a word that is horrendous enough. This horrific disease took the lives of three very important people in my life. Thankfully, the loss is only temporary.

I have always believed in God, but I truly did not know a relationship with Him until my mom was diagnosed in June 2005 with bladder cancer. She was an amazing lady. She taught us how to love, how to be kind, and how to trust that God loved us and would always provide.

Her electric blue eyes, amazing smile, and unbelievable laugh will be with me forever, and thinking of her beautiful life brings tears stinging to my eyes even after all this time. She was the core of our family who held us all together, and cancer took her earthly body from us. It wrought havoc on her mind and body as well as on the emotions of everyone who loved her.

Shortly before her passing, I had a conversation with her and told her it was okay to let go. We loved her with all of our hearts and wanted her to get better, but her suffering had become unbearable for her and for all of us who loved her. We just wanted her to be out of the pain and misery she had suffered for so long. She seemed to be holding on for reasons we did not understand and enduring pain that seemed inhuman, knowing deep down her time would be short. She had a tracheotomy at the time, so communicating was very difficult for her.

When I said this to her, her face become troubled and her breathing quickened. Her eyes looked as though she was in physical pain. As tears welled in her eyes, I asked what was wrong. She told me, "I can't let go until I know all of my kids know God." I remember thinking to myself, 'Well of course, we believe in God, why would you even worry about this?' As the saying goes, if I had known then what I know now.

This makes a lot more sense to me now that I have been born again. Wanting to reassure her and give her peace, I explained to her that she did not need to worry about us, that we would be fine, and that we did know God. She continued to have this urgency in her eyes that I will never forget. She was not convinced all of her children were saved. She made me promise in that moment that I would do everything in my power to make sure we all knew God. She knew where she was headed. She was not fearful of where she was going because Jesus Christ resided in her heart. She knew she was going home.

Her fear came in not knowing whether she would see us again. She was always thinking with a mom's heart. She eventually gave it over to God, as she had done with so many of her worries over the years, and she went to be with Jesus two weeks before the celebration of His birth. My journey toward God took a giant leap forward.

In 2008, my sister's husband lost a long battle to cancer. It originated in the lungs, went into remission, and resurfaced with a vengeance in the pancreas. Let me just say, the symptoms involved with both of these cancers are, simply put, made for horror movies. The intense pain in your digestive system, the inability to eat, drink, or get comfortable combined with the anxiety of not breathing well all add to the fact that you know your time is being cut short because what you have is terminal.

It is difficult for me even to think about, let alone endure. It took his life at 51. He always believed there was a higher power at large and in control, but this journey with cancer brought him to the cross and he allowed Jesus into his heart and is now where he belongs -- at home. God is an awesome God. The pain of Dan's passing ripped open wounds that had not yet healed from my mom dying and left our family emotionally raw. He left behind his wife of 25 years, his 16-year-old son, and his 11-year-old daughter to try to find a way to go on. My friend and her children who are like my own left alone to fend for themselves..

I found myself thinking, "How do you find your identity again when you have given the other half of it to someone who is now gone with no return? How do you find your smile again?" I know people go through this kind of loss every day, but how do you cope when it's happening to you? I know we all are going to die someday, but this just isn't right. It just doesn't seem fair. Thankfully, I later found answers to all of those questions and much, much more.

Fast forward to June 2010 when my dad was diagnosed with lung cancer that had spread to other parts of his body. The doctor gave him three months to live with no treatment and six 6 months at best with treatment. Imagine, after everything we all had been through, a doctor, as nonchalantly as if he is talking about the weather, tells you if you choose no treatment you may have three months to live, and if you choose chemo, you will endure the painful symptoms of the treatment during most of the time you have left. Now I know God has the ultimate say in our time here on Earth, but these can't possibly be the only options, can they? With regard to the doctor's demeanor, keep in mind that my dad was a long-time heavy smoker, a functioning alcohol, and on Medicaid.

Needless to say, the doctor felt my dad got what was coming to him and said as much. Thankfully, God felt differently. My dad was a loving, smart, and creative man. He always loved me, encouraged me, and taught me how to persevere in things I was passionate about. Unfortunately, his addiction took over many aspects of his life, destroying relationships, leaving him broken and alone. It took this death sentence to truly open his eyes to the love God had for him and the joy and blessings that come with receiving Jesus into his heart. He mended important relations (ours was one of them), truly humbled himself, saw his sin, and asked for God's forgiveness.

This was something he had never done with a genuine heart. God was truly glorified through my dad's death in more ways than I have time to explain. Dad was a broken, addicted man living in fear and sin, terrified of death, putting his own wants before living for God. Through his experience with cancer, he became a man who knew that death was not to be feared but to be welcomed because it meant he was going home to a Father who loves, forgives, protects and who laid down his life for him, unlike his earthly father who abused him and left him broken. My dad passed away on Christmas Day with peace in his spirit and love in his heart. My journey toward God is now at a running pace.

Cancer is hateful. When I think of it, I see Satan's face all over it. It is a clear representation of his very essence. Cancer lies, it hides in the shadows, and resurfaces when you least expect it. It seeks to destroy everything good in its path; it literally must devour, mutate, and destroy good cells in order to thrive. It chooses victims with a weakness in their body systems, begins with one tiny cell, invades the body, and transforms what is good and healthy into a deadly weapon. It does this one cell at a time, spreading to the rest of the body, persevering until it destroys it.

There is no real understanding of why cancer occurs or how to stop it permanently. I know there are things we do to our bodies that raise the risk of getting cancer, but cancer can invade the most innocent of creatures who have not done any purposeful harm to their bodies, some who have not even been alive long enough to be exposed to these types of things. We are talking about one cell that hides in your body for an unknown amount of time, learning how to mimic what is good in the body in order to remain hidden in the body until it is ready to take over and begin its destruction.

Not only that, but when the body goes into remission and it appears the cancer has disappeared, it comes back in a different part of the body with a vengeance. I mean, seriously, think about how evil and deceitful this is. It is a living, breathing, monster that invades our bodies without our even knowing and destroys our earthly bodies, bodies that were fearfully and wonderfully made. Does this sound familiar to anyone? Does it remind you of anyone in particular?

Here is the good news. The questions I had been asking myself about why this was happening to us, what was the point in all of this, why did we have to endure such pain and heartache? Why was God allowing so much pain, and the biggest question of all," What else did He want from us and specifically me?" Funny question that is because He wanted all of me, all of us.

The only way that was going to happen was to allow us to go through these trials and heartache so we would come to Him. He was willing to endure the pain of watching His children hurt, crying with us, hurting with us, and wishing there was another way this could be accomplished but knowing it would be worth the sacrifice in the end. He allowed the pain and suffering because He knew I would finally come to him with arms and heart wide open, receiving his love and wanting to serve Him with all of my heart.

He knew what it would take to change this stubborn heart of mine and the hearts of my family. He created me and knows me better than I know myself, and in order for me to truly change, it was going to have to hurt. What an awesome and loving God who would have such patience, love, mercy, and grace to mold a sinner like me into a child of His Kingdom, believing I am worthy enough to serve Him and fulfill the purpose He has for me.

I am quite sure Satan trembles at this thought. How amazing that God is never late. He gathered his three children just in time before they reached the point of no return, scooping them up in His arms to take them home. My experience with cancer has changed my life forever. My life could have taken a turn in so many different destructive directions, but God was persistent and, being the jealous God He is, He was not going to let Satan win me or my loved ones. What Satan intended to destroy, God renewed. God won…God always wins. You just have to choose to believe it.

This is how you go on, how you find your smile, and how you continue to love; you live your life for God having accepted Jesus Christ into your heart as your Lord and Savior, serving the Lord as you wait patiently to be with Him in Paradise, taking as many people with you as you can to an eternal place in God's presence where Satan and his cancer will never be allowed to enter.

Marv and Tarry Everingham Story

What kind of cancer did you have?

Early in 1994 I noticed a lump under my left jaw. Went to the doctor. He says, let's watch it for a month. Probably just a swollen gland. He gave me an antibiotic. A month later, the lump was still there and had grown. The doctor sent me to an oncologist, and it was confirmed by biopsy that I had non-Hodgkins lymphoma.

What kind of treatment did you receive?

I started out with chemo called CHOP for 36 weeks. Back then it's about all they had. It is a devastating and debilitating chemo. I would have chemo on Fridays, puke all weekend/ and go back to work on Monday. After the first two treatments they finally gave me some meds with the chemo to lessen the vomiting and sick stomach. It was miserable. I could hardly make it through the day at work and would come home and literally crash in my recliner until time for bed arrived.

After the 36 weeks, they said we had to wait a couple months to see whether or not it worked. Within three months, it was back, and I started chemo treatments. The cancer came back within two months after the treatment, so I started chemo treatments once again. After the third session was finished and the cancer came back, the doctors told me there was nothing else they could do. That is when we asked for a referral to the Mayo Clinic.

We were treated like royalty at the Mayo Clinic. After being there only three days, they recommended a new chemo drug that showed promise. They contacted my doctor with instructions, and I began that treatment. It was much easier than the first three rounds and didn't make me nearly as sick. This was in 1998, as I recall.

Shortly thereafter, the cancer returned. We were given the choice of repeating the same chemo or trying a new experimental drug made from ocean algae. We decided to try the experimental chemo even though we had to travel from Onaway area (up near the Mackinac Bridge) to Detroit for it. We did this for about six months. The experimental chemo caused horrendous leg cramps. I would literally fall to the ground and roll around in pain until they eased up. We quit the treatment shortly after that.

We moved back downstate in 2000, and within a couple months, the cancer was back. By that time, we had transferred to a new doctor in Grand Rapids. Dr. Zakem had a relatively new chemo that showed some success. We tried it, and it worked! I was cancer free for about three years and thought the battle had been won. Little did we know that things started to change little by little in 2003. Within a short time, it was back to chemo again.

This went on until late 2006 when things took a change for the worse. My blood counts were going down fast. Dr. Zakem did a bone marrow draw and discovered that I had gone from lymphoma to myelodysplastic syndrome. At that time, I was being kept alive by blood transfusions at least twice a week. The doctor spoke of a possible bone marrow transplant but thought I was too old to survive it. Following our strong insistence,, he referred us to the BMT UNIT at University of Michigan.

We met with specialists and began testing etc. to locate a donor. By May 2007, I had been hospitalized many times with various conditions, the last of which was MRSA. I was in Butterworth Hospital in Grand Rapids. On his rounds one morning, Dr. Zakem started out with, "Marv and Tarry, I really hate to have to have this conversation, but if your labs continue to go in the direction they are going, you will most likely be in a coma by tomorrow and then die. I suggest you get your affairs in order and have your family come." It didn't look like he was going to live long enough to be use Aeromed [helicopter ride] to Ann Arbor for the transplant even though a perfect donor had been found.

Can you describe the feelings and emotions you or your loved one/family had when the doctor confirmed you had cancer?

Waiting for the official word from the original biopsy was worse than knowing that it was cancer. It took about five days back then for the confirmation. We were supposed to go camping for a week right then. The doctor said to go ahead, have a great time, and he'd see me when we got back. Right!!!! That was the worst vacation we ever had. Couldn't sleep, couldn't unwind or have much fun. Cancer was constantly on our minds.

What kinds of things are you doing to help yourself to relax or find support?

The thing that bothered us at first was that many people we considered friends suddenly became Non-existent. It's like they were afraid they would catch it. This hurta lot! There were very few people we considered real friends after this initial shock. The biggest thing that helped us was turning closer to God and His word. We clung to our church family up north. Because we didn't have any family living there, they became our family. Complete strangers took me to Detroit for treatments. In fact, a couple was on vacation from Ohio came to our church one Sunday. It was announced that I needed a ride to Detroit for chemo that week, and the lady of the family called us and volunteered to take me. She actually sacrificed a day of her vacation for a complete stranger!! This was no coincidence. God put her in our church that morning for a reason.

Then once we moved back down here in 2000 and began attending GCC, a floodgate of close friends became known to us. Our church family is more than a church family; our church family is our FAMILY!!! You all know who you are. We have had so many wonderful things done for us such as rides to doctor appointments in Ann Arbor or to GR for testing, people helping us move from Miles Road to Sidney Road, and helping get the house ready to move into. Pastor Tom and Val even loaned us their camper to live in while we were at Ann Arbor. Our small group is the very best. We couldn't make it through the week without them. We all love each other so much and try to show the love of Jesus to others. Our church FAMILY even had a fundraiser for us before we went to Ann Arbor for four months for the transplant.

We relax with friends, read the Bible, and pray every day. We are so thankful for so Many things. Marv and Tarry's most relaxing times are fishing on the pontoon. It's just the three of us--God, Marv, and Tarry. We praise Him and thank Him every time we go out.

During the journey, do you recall times when you questioned God and His plan?

Of course. We would be lying if we didn't. Because we are human, we always have to ask why? Why me? Why now? What do you want me to learn from this? Once we got over the initial shock, we discovered we don't need to know why and that in many ways this cancer has been a huge blessing. It has brought us both closer to God and totally dependent on Him. In fact, we find that the best way to deal with Marv's physical inconveniences is to reach out and help others. We have done that many times and will continue as long as God gives us breath.

Were there any Scripture, songs, or music you leaned on for comfort and strength?

One song that has been very comforting to both of us is "I Can Only Imagine," and when Darren Signs sings it so beautifully, it brings tears to our eyes. "Amazing Grace" has also been a comfort. Marv falls back to Matthew 7:7 which says, "Keep on asking, and you will be given what you ask for. Keep on looking, and you will find. Keep on knocking, and the door will be opened." Tarry has had great comfort from reading the book When God Doesn't Heal Now by Larry Keefauver. It was given to her by a friend when Marv was first diagnosed. It helped her realize that even if God doesn't heal Marv on this side of Heaven, it Is okay. She can accept that and have peace knowing he is finally healed and free of pain.

How did your relationship with Christ change?

Marv - My relationship was not real. I have gone from nothing to everything. I depend on God for all things. He sets my days and my nights. I say to Him every morning, "Thank you, Lord, for another day on your beautiful Earth."

Tarry - I had a flirting relationship with Christ until sometime in 1982. It was then that I became serious and asked Him to take control of my life. He has blessed me way beyond measure. I thank Him for the beautiful sunrises and sunsets, for the rainbows, for the wonderful times at the lake we both love. I thank Him for family and friends and for dying for my sins. I will forever lift HIM higher. We both feel that He let all these challenges happen to us to keep us close and to keep us humble. For that we are eternally grateful.

Barb Vickery Story

What Kind of cancer did you have?

Breast cancer, beginning state, caught early

What kind of treatment did you or your loved one receive?

Surgery to remove spot, chemo, Herceptin, radiation (32)

Can you describe the feelings and emotions you felt when the doctor confirmed you had cancer?

Doubt

During the journey, do you recall times when you questioned God and His plan?

Yes, when so many people were praying and I became sicker and sicker.

Were there Scriptures, songs, or music you leaned on for comfort and strength?

Trust in the Lord with all your heart, with all your soul, and with all your mind.

How did your relationship with Christ change?

I had to climb up on His lap one day. When this is all over, I will get back down, but right now it is where I need to be.

Credits and References

Poem 3 – Christianity Today - http://www.christianitytoday.com/ct/2013/november/fox-news-highly-reluctant-jesus-follower-kirsten-powers.html

Poem 5 - Charity Toxic Charity: How the Church Hurts Those They Help and How to Reverse It by Robert Lupton - ISBN-10: 0062076213 or ISBN-13: 978-0062076212

Poem 16 - Heaven Is for Real by Todd Burpo and Lynn Vincent ISBN-10: 0849946158 or ISBN-13: 978-0849946158

Poem 16 - 90 Minutes in Heaven: A True Story of Death and Life by Don Piper, Cecil Murphey ISBN-10: 0800759494 or ISBN-13: 978-0800759490

Poem 17 – The books of the Bible - Biblica, Inc. ISBN-10: 1563206609 ISBN-13: 978-1563206603

Poem 19 – "Noah" the movie http://www.imdb.com/title/tt1959490/

Poem 21 - The Duck Commander Devotional by Alan Robertson ISBN-10: 1476748683 or ISBN-13: 978-1476748689

Poem 22 - Unthinkable by Scott Rigsby and Jenna Glatzer ISBN-10: 1414333145 or ISBN-13: 978-1414333144

Shavonne Smith's story - You Can Be Healed by Billy Jo Daugherty ISBN-10: 0892748761 or ISBN-13: 978-0892748761

List of Original "C" words

Change
Children
Conquer
Cross
Creativity
Courage
Conviction
Contrite
Cherish
Contentment
Caring
Cultivate
Conversion
Compassion
Clean
Consistency
Clear
Comfortable
Christ
Charity
Church
Cash
Challenge
Command
Credit
Cry
Convey
Community
Comfort
Cleanse
Communion
Captive

Crown
Center
Come
Cushion
Calm
Crowd
Climb
Collaborative
Confident
Celebration

About the Author

Steve Schofield was saved in August 2005, and began writing poems shortly after to deal with life's stresses. He lives in West Michigan with his wife Cindy and together they have three grown sons. They are active members at Greenville (MI) Community Church.

Steve is an IT professional and a self-described "internet geek," he used that skill to develop a couple of online applications that fund his writing habit. He is the author of other Christian devotionals:

52 Pickup: These Are the Words I Give to You to Share with Everyone (ISBN-13: 978-1449773045)

- Paperback – http://amzn.to/UiExjv
- Kindle Version - http://amzn.to/10q38W1

Remember the Nails: 40 Days of Doing Something Uncomfortable on Purpose (ISBN-13 : **978-0-9979021-1-2**)

One Reason: 21 Days to a new Beginning (ISBN-13 : **978-0-9979021-0-5**)

All glory goes to God for using these poems and stories. He has inspired me to share them. There certainly is nothing like having our Creator speak directly to you. Words can't describe it! I only hope I can help others along their own paths towards Christ.

Visit http://www.ponderingthought.com for latest information on Steve's books.